Determining the Effectiveness of Campus Services

Robert A. Scott, *Editor*

NEW DIRECTIONS FOR INSTITUTIONAL RESEARCH
Sponsored by the Association for Institutional Research
MARVIN W. PETERSON, PATRICK T. TERENZINI
Editors-in-Chief

Number 41, March 1984

Paperback sourcebooks in
The Jossey-Bass Higher Education Series

Jossey-Bass Inc., Publishers
San Francisco • Washington • London

Robert A. Scott (Ed.).
Determining the Effectiveness of Campus Services.
New Directions for Institutional Research, no. 41.
Volume XI, number 1.
San Francisco: Jossey-Bass, 1984.

New Directions for Institutional Research Series
Marvin W. Peterson, Patrick T. Terenzini, *Editors-in-Chief*

Copyright © 1984 by Jossey-Bass Inc., Publishers
                    and
                    Jossey-Bass Limited

Copyright under International, Pan American, and Universal
Copyright Conventions. All rights reserved. No part of
this issue may be reproduced in any form — except for brief
quotation (not to exceed 500 words) in a review or professional
work — without permission in writing from the publishers.

New Directions for Institutional Research (publication number
USPS 098-830) is published quarterly by Jossey-Bass Inc.,
Publishers, and is sponsored by the Association for Institutional
Research. The volume and issue numbers above are included for
the convenience of libraries. Second-class postage rates paid at
San Francisco, California, and at additional mailing offices.

Correspondence:
Subscriptions, single-issue orders, change of address notices, undelivered
copies, and other correspondence should be sent to Subscriptions,
Jossey-Bass Inc., Publishers, 433 California Street, San Francisco
California 94104.

Editorial correspondence should be sent to the Editor-in-Chief,
Marvin W. Peterson, Center for the Study of Higher Education,
University of Michigan, Ann Arbor, Michigan 48109, or
Patrick T. Terenzini, Office of Institutional Research, SUNY,
Albany, New York 12222.

Library of Congress Catalogue Card Number LC 83-82727
International Standard Serial Number ISSN 0271-0579
International Standard Book Number ISBN 87589-999-4

Cover art by Willi Baum
Manufactured in the United States of America

Ordering Information

The paperback sourcebooks listed below are published quarterly and can be ordered either by subscription or single-copy.
Subscriptions cost $35.00 per year for institutions, agencies, and libraries. Individuals can subscribe at the special rate of $25.00 per year *if payment is by personal check*. (Note that the full rate of $35.00 applies if payment is by institutional check, even if the subscription is designated for an individual.) Standing orders are accepted. Subscriptions normally begin with the first of the four sourcebooks in the current publication year of the series. When ordering, please indicate if you prefer your subscription to begin with the first issue of the *coming* year.
Single copies are available at $8.95 when payment accompanies order, and *all single-copy orders under $25.00 must include payment*. (California, New Jersey, New York, and Washington, D.C., residents please include appropriate sales tax.) For billed orders, cost per copy is $8.95 plus postage and handling. (Prices subject to change without notice.)
Bulk orders (ten or more copies) of any individual sourcebook are available at the following discounted prices: 10-49 copies, $8.05 each; 50-100 copies, $7.15 each; over 100 copies, *inquire*. Sales tax and postage and handling charges apply as for single copy orders.
To ensure correct and prompt delivery, all orders must give either the *name of an individual* or an *official purchase order number*. Please submit your order as follows:

Subscriptions: specify series and year subscription is to begin.
Single Copies: specify sourcebook code (such as, IR8) and first two words of title.

Mail orders for United States and Possessions, Latin America, Canada, Japan, Australia, and New Zealand to:
Jossey-Bass Inc., Publishers
433 California Street
San Francisco, California 94104

Mail orders for all other parts of the world to:
Jossey-Bass Limited
28 Banner Street
London EC1Y 8QE

New Directions for Institutional Research Series
Marvin W. Peterson, Patrick T. Terenzini
Editors-in-Chief

IR1 *Evaluating Institutions for Accountability,* Howard R. Bowen
IR2 *Assessing Faculty Effort,* James I. Doi
IR3 *Toward Affirmative Action,* Lucy W. Sells
IR4 *Organizing Nontraditional Study,* Samuel Baskin

IR5   *Evaluating Statewide Boards,* Robert O. Berdahl
IR6   *Assuring Academic Progress Without Growth,* Allan M. Cartter
IR7   *Responding to Changing Human Resource Needs,* Paul Heist, Jonathan R. Warren
IR8   *Measuring and Increasing Academic Productivity,* Robert A. Wallhaus
IR9   *Assessing Computer-Based System Models,* Thomas R. Mason
IR10 *Examining Departmental Management,* James Smart, James Montgomery
IR11 *Allocating Resources Among Departments,* Paul L. Dressel, Lou Anna Kimsey Simon
IR12 *Benefiting from Interinstitutional Research,* Marvin W. Peterson
IR13 *Applying Analytic Methods to Planning and Management,* David S. P. Hopkins, Roger G. Schroeder
IR14 *Protecting Individual Rights to Privacy in Higher Education,* Alton L. Taylor
IR15 *Appraising Information Needs of Decision Makers,* Carl R. Adams
IR16 *Increasing the Public Accountability of Higher Education,* John K. Folger
IR17 *Analyzing and Constructing Cost,* Meredith A. Gonyea
IR18 *Employing Part-Time Faculty,* David W. Leslie
IR19 *Using Goals in Research and Planning,* Robert Fenske
IR20 *Evaluating Faculty Performance and Vitality,* Wayne C. Kirschling
IR21 *Developing a Total Marketing Plan,* John A. Lucas
IR22 *Examining New Trends in Administrative Computing,* E. Michael Staman
IR23 *Professional Development for Institutional Research,* Robert G. Cope
IR24 *Planning Rational Retrenchment,* Alfred L. Cooke
IR25 *The Impact of Student Financial Aid on Institutions,* Joe B. Henry
IR26 *The Autonomy of Public Colleges,* Paul L. Dressel
IR27 *Academic Program Evaluation,* Eugene C. Craven
IR28 *Academic Planning for the 1980s,* Richard B. Heydinger
IR29 *Institutional Assessment for Self-Improvement,* Richard I. Miller
IR30 *Coping with Faculty Reduction,* Stephen R. Hample
IR31 *Evaluation of Management and Planning Systems,* Nick L. Poulton
IR32 *Increasing the Use of Program Evaluation,* Jack Lindquist
IR33 *Effective Planned Change Strategies,* G. Melvin Hipps
IR34 *Qualitative Methods for Institutional Research,* Eileen Kuhns, S. V. Martorana
IR35 *Information Technology: Advances and Applications,* Bernard Sheehan
IR36 *Studying Student Attrition,* Ernest T. Pascarella
IR37 *Using Research for Strategic Planning,* Norman P. Uhl
IR38 *The Politics and Pragmatics of Institutional Research,* James W. Firnberg, William F. Lasher
IR39 *Applying Methods and Techniques of Futures Research,* James L. Morrison, William L. Renfro, Wayne I. Boucher
IR40 *College Faculty: Versatile Human Resources in a Period of Constraint,* Roger G. Baldwin, Robert T. Blackburn

Contents

Editor's Notes 1
Robert A. Scott

Chapter 1. Enhancing Campus Quality Through Self-Study 9
Robert H. Chambers
The institutional self-study is a unique instrument for assessing and enhancing institutional effectiveness.

Chapter 2. Assessing the Quality of Student Services 23
Joseph F. Kauffman
Student services may be more crucial to higher education institutions than ever before.

Chapter 3. Assessing the Performance of the Public Relations Office 37
Carol P. Halstead
Public relations can be effective, but it must be planned with objectives and assessed with rigor.

Chapter 4. Higher Education and Industry: Planning and Assessing the New Alliance 51
Susan Powell
The New Economy calls for new alliances between education and industry which must be organized in a manner that makes it possible to evaluate them.

Chapter 5. Evaluating the Effectiveness of Academic Libraries and Computing Facilities 61
Donald R. Brown, Shirley M. Smith, with Robert A. Scott
The principal academic support services of an institution are difficult to evaluate: When is enough enough?

Chapter 6. Assessing Institutional Ineffectiveness: A Strategy for Improvement 67
Kim S. Cameron
Negative performance feedback is a necessary precondition for organizational improvement.

Chapter 7. Concluding Notes and Further Readings 85
Robert A. Scott

Index 89

The Association for Institutional Research was created in 1966 to benefit, assist, and advance research leading to improved understanding, planning, and operation of institutions of higher education. Publication policy is set by its Publications Board.

PUBLICATIONS BOARD
Marilyn McCoy (Chairperson), University of Colorado System
Jean J. Endo, University of Colorado–Boulder
William P. Fenstemacher, University of Massachusetts–Boston
Stephen R. Hample, Montana State University
Richard B. Heydinger, University of Minnesota
Penny A. Wallhaus, Illinois Community College Board

EX-OFFICIO MEMBERS OF THE PUBLICATIONS BOARD
Daniel R. Coleman, University of Central Florida
Charles F. Elton, University of Kentucky
Gerald W. McLaughlin, Virginia Polytechnic Institute & State University
Marvin W. Peterson, University of Michigan

EDITORIAL ADVISORY BOARD
All members of the Publications Board and:
Frederick E. Balderston, University of California, Berkeley
Howard R. Bowen, Claremont Graduate School
Roberta D. Brown, Arkansas College
Lyman A. Glenny, University of California, Berkeley
David S. P. Hopkins, Stanford University
Roger G. Schroeder, University of Minnesota
Robert J. Silverman, Ohio State University
Martin A. Trow, University of California, Berkeley

For information about the Association for Institutional Research, write:

> AIR Executive Office
> 314 Stone Building
> Florida State University
> Tallahassee, FL 32306
>
> (904)644-4470

Editor's Notes

The purpose of this sourcebook is to offer college and university officials and faculty leaders practical approaches to assessing the performance of campus services. It is only by evaluating the effectiveness of such services that campus leaders can best fulfill their roles as stewards, managers, and leaders. This, then, is a sourcebook for those who will appoint individuals and committees to design and conduct the evaluation of selected campus services, as well as for those who will serve on such committees.

While the criteria by which services are evaluated will vary by campus type, by type of student enrollment, and by other campus characteristics, the kinds of considerations and forms of evidence of effectiveness are universal. In order to evaluate the effectiveness of performance, we must understand the purposes or goals of the activity or service, the congruence between service goals and institutional goals, efficiency in the use of resources, the context in which the service, program, or other activity takes place, and the degree to which the service or function attains its goals and objectives. Its effectiveness may be said to approach excellence when it has achieved superior attainment of distinctive objectives (Scott, 1980–81).

According to Lehmann (1981), evaluation has four key features: (1) the provision of accurate, timely, reliable, and valid information, which assumes that the evaluation process includes a research strategy and an evaluation framework; (2) the determination that a given service or program is operating in such a way as to achieve its objectives, which implies the use of certain standards for assessing the success of the program; (3) information that is useful to administrative and faculty decision-makers so that the results of the evaluation can make meaningful contributions to improving the service and the institution; and (4) service outcomes that are related to costs, which suggests that cost data are an integral part of the evaluation effort even when cost data are considered after service objectives and outcomes have been determined.

Much has been written about faculty, administrator, and program evaluation. There is a rich literature on each of these topics, and thus they do not receive much attention in this volume. However, there are some campus services that are also important but whose evaluation has not received sufficient attention. These topics include: accreditation self-studies and the relationship of these reports to campus planning, student services, an institution's ability to communicate with its publics about its special strengths, university public service and technical assistance partnerships with corporations, and such academic services as libraries and computing facilities. The purpose of the chapters in this volume is to assist senior and mid-level university administrators and faculty leaders in defining and developing procedures for assessing the quality of these services.

Measures of Organizational Effectiveness

One of the first questions to be asked when discussing organizational effectiveness is: Who defines effectiveness? After all, effectiveness can be considered the product of individual values and preferences. In a college or university, those who are concerned about effectiveness include all those directly associated with the institution as well as potential students, parents of potential students, potential faculty, potential funders, graduate school admissions committees, employers, peer review panels, and accreditation peers. These parties represent a diversity of concerns; thus, when considering the effectiveness of performance, one must keep in mind the answer to the question, effectiveness according to whom? We usually mean effectiveness according to some group other than those performing the services.

The specific criteria by which we measure effectiveness vary not only according to individual values and preferences, but also by type of organization. Whether an institution is public or private, unionized or nonunionized, large or small, two-year or four-year, a research university, early in its development or mature in organization will influence the ways in which we consider its effectiveness.

The variety of persons who make judgments about effectiveness and the variety of considerations they employ lead some analysts to conclude that it is not clear what constitutes optimal performance in higher education. Cameron (1983, p. 39) comments on this:

> This condition of ambiguity regarding what constitutes effective performance is characteristic of colleges and universities. These organizations not only are typified by an absence of measurable goals, loose coupling, little direct connection between acquired resources and products, an ability to ignore major constituencies, and so on, (Cameron, 1978, 1980), but they have a tradition of resistance to assessment of effectiveness that has kept consensual criteria of effectiveness from emerging. Colleges and universities argue fervently that they are unlike other types of organizations, and therefore that traditional approaches to assessment are not applicable (March and Olsen, 1976; Weick, 1976). The uniqueness of each institution is also argued to make comparative assessments among schools questionable (Dressel, 1971). Whereas judgments about college and university effectiveness must occur regularly by accreditation agencies, potential students and faculty members, parents, funders, and employers, no good criteria of effectiveness have ever been identified, and the meaning of effectiveness in higher education is unclear (Hutchins, 1977). It is not that attempts haven't been made to identify criteria, it is just that the indicators of effectiveness selected by researchers have brought little clarity to the construct.

In order to bring further clarity to the subject, Cameron studied the responses from a sample of institutions to questions about institutional characteristics. The questionnaire was designed to solicit descriptions, but the composite of answers, together with other data, permitted Cameron to assess nine separate dimensions of institutional effectiveness. These dimensions are summarized in Table 1 (Cameron, 1983, p. 39). According to Cameron (1983, p. 15), these predictor variables were used because they have been found to be associated with performance in other types of organizations. These same nine dimensions of effectiveness also have emerged in other research. Both internal and external validities of the measures are reported to be high (Cameron, 1983, pp. 16, 18).

In conclusion, Cameron cites the following findings (1983, pp. 21-22):

Table 1. Nine Dimensions of Organizational Effectiveness in Institutions of Higher Education

Dimension	*Definition*
1. Student Educational Satisfaction	The extent to which students are satisfied with their educational experiences at the institution.
2. Student Academic Development	The extent of the academic growth, attainment, and progress of students at the institution.
3. Student Career Development	The extent of occupational preparedness of the students, and the emphasis on career development provided by the institution.
4. Student Personal Development	The extent of student development in nonacademic, noncareer oriented areas, and the emphasis on personal development provided by the school.
5. Faculty and Administrator Employment Satisfaction	The extent of satisfaction of faculty members and administrators with their employment at the institution.
6. Professional Development and Quality of the Faculty	The extent of professional attainment and development of the faculty, and the emphasis on development provided by the institution.
7. System Openness and Community Interaction	The extent of interaction with, adaptation to, and services provided for the external environment by the institution.
8. Ability to Acquire Resources	The ability of the institution to acquire needed resources such as high quality students and faculty, financial support, etc.
9. Organizational Health	The extent to which the internal processes and practices in the institution are smooth functioning and benevolent.

These findings indicate that for every dimension of effectiveness, the strategic emphasis of top institutional administrators is significantly related to high scores. A strategic emphasis by top administrators on academic and scholarly affairs, for example, is associated with high effectiveness on four dimensions—student educational satisfaction, student academic development, professional development and quality of the faculty, and organizational health. Implementing strategies proactively, instead of reactively, is associated with high scores on three of the dimensions—faculty and administrator employment satisfaction, system openness and community interaction, and ability to acquire resources. A strategic emphasis on public service, student affairs, and fund raising are associated with two effectiveness dimensions each. In brief, of all the categories of variables assessed, the most powerful factors associated with organizational effectiveness in these institutions of higher education tend to be those under the control of managers. That is, managers' strategic emphases, their stance toward proactivity rather than reactivity, and the quality of students they can attract are among the most influential variables in predicting to what extent the institutions score high on the effectiveness dimensions. Environmental turbulence, a largely uncontrolled factor, appears to be the major constraint on performance.

Because of Cameron's studies, we now have a better understanding of organizational effectiveness in colleges and universities. According to him, the most important factors associated with organizational effectiveness are those under the control of organizational leaders and managers.

Criteria for the Selection of Topics

When given the opportunity to edit a volume on assessing the effectiveness of performance of college and university services and functions, one has to decide which services and functions to address. There are several criteria to consider in this selection process. University activities are generally thought of as either primary, including instruction, research, and public service, or secondary, including student services, administrative services, and auxiliary enterprises. This distinction is derived from the conclusion that the first set of activities includes the principal functions of a college or university and the second set is supportive of the first. Therefore, because of their importance, one might select instruction, research, and public service as the functions whose effectiveness is to be addressed.

Another view is that one should give the most attention to those functions for which expenditures are the greatest. For the past decade at least, approximately one third of annual campus expenditures has gone to instruction, about 10 percent to research, and about 3 percent to public service, with the remainder (about 55 percent) spent on support activities (American Council on Education, 1982). By this criterion, instruction should receive the most attention from evaluators because it is the single most costly function. Still another view is that an examination of effectiveness should be devoted to those activities in which an institution has the greatest investment in professional staff. This view considers the professional staff as the chief asset of a college or university and suggests that most attention should be devoted to the areas of instruction, research, and administration.

We have reviewed the literature on evaluation and measures of effectiveness and have concluded that there exists a substantial amount of material that reports the theories and practices of faculty, program, and administrative evaluation. In fact, the literature on these areas is so extensive, although not of uniformly high quality, that it was deemed unnecessary and undesirable to produce a new volume. Therefore, we have limited ourselves to calling attention to the important and useful works that have reviewed this literature and identified practices for the evaluation of these functions. For this volume, we have decided to focus on areas of function and service that meet two criteria: They have not received a great deal of attention in the literature, and they seem highly susceptible to administrative action and improvement. Cameron's work cited earlier supports our selection of topics. We have chosen topics that are susceptible to administrative direction and whose effectiveness affects how people perceive an institution. The topics of teaching, faculty, staff, program, and research evaluation have been omitted from consideration in this sourcebook because they are well covered in other volumes. Selected sources of information about the ways in which these functions are evaluated may be found in the selected bibliography at the end of this chapter.

A Brief Review of the Chapters

Each chapter was written by an accomplished professional who has provided references to appropriate literature and guidance on developing procedures. Lynn Barnett, assistant director of the ERIC Clearinghouse on Higher Education, served as research consultant for the authors.

In Chapter One, Robert H. Chambers, dean of the College of Arts and Sciences at Bucknell University and a frequent participant in and chair of regional accrediting reviews, discusses how to assess the quality of accreditation self-studies and how such reports can be incorporated into institutional plans for continuing development and evaluation.

Joseph Kauffman, professor of educational administration and former executive vice-president of the University of Wisconsin System, writes in Chapter Two on assessing the quality of performance of student services.

Chapter Three, written by Carol Halstead, president of College Connections, Inc., and former director of public relations for the College Entrance Examination Board, discusses assessing the quality of an institution's communications with its publics about its special strengths.

In Chapter Four, Susan Powell, manager of research and evaluation at

McGraw-Hill Book Company and former director of academic planning and program review for the Minnesota Council on Higher Education, addresses the topic of assessing the performance of university public service and technical assistance partnerships with corporations.

Chapter Five, by Donald R. Brown, vice-president and dean for academic services at Purdue University, and Shirley M. Smith, assistant dean of academic services at Purdue, offers a brief statement on assessing the quality of performance of academic libraries and computer facilities. This section was developed in abbreviated form with the assistance of the editor, because illness interrupted the work of the senior author.

In Chapter Six, Kim S. Cameron, director of organizational studies at the National Center for Higher Education Management Systems, provides a provocative essay on the use of negative performance feedback for improving institutional effectiveness.

Robert A. Scott
Editor

References

American Council on Education. *1981-82 Fact Book.* Washington, D.C.: American Council on Education, 1982.

Cameron, K. "Measuring Organizational Effectiveness in Institutions of Higher Education." *Admininstrative Science Quarterly,* 1978, *23,* 604-632.

Cameron, K. "Critical Questions in Assessing Organizational Effectiveness." *Organizational Dynamics,* 1980, *9,* 66-80.

Cameron, K. *A Study of Organizational Effectiveness and Its Predictors.* Boulder, Colo.: National Center for Higher Education Management Systems, 1983.

Digest of Education Statistics. Washington, D.C.: National Center for Education Statistics, 1982.

Dressel, P. *The New Colleges: Toward An Appraisal.* Iowa City: American College Testing Program and American Association of Higher Education, 1971.

Hutchins, R. "Interview with Robert Maynard Hutchins." *Chronicle of Higher Education,* 1977, *14,* 5.

Lehmann, T. "Evaluating Adult Learning and Program Costs." In A. Chickering and Associates (Eds.), *The Modern American College: Responding to the New Realities of Diverse Students and a Changing Society.* San Francisco: Jossey-Bass, 1981.

March, J., and Olsen, J. *Ambiguity and Choice in Organizations.* Oslo, Norway: Universitetsforlaget, 1976.

Scott, R. A. "Quality: Program Review's Missing Link." *The College Board Review,* Winter 1980-81, *118,* 18-21, 30.

Weick, K. "Educational Organizations as Loosely Coupled Systems." *Administrative Science Quarterly,* 1976, *21,* 1-19.

Selected Bibliography

Evaluation of Faculty

Centra, J. A. *Determining Faculty Effectiveness.* San Francisco: Jossey-Bass, 1979.

Kirschling, W. R. (Ed.). *Evaluating Faculty Performance and Vitality.* New Directions for Institutional Research, no. 20. San Francisco: Jossey-Bass, 1978.

Evaluation of Administration

Fisher, C. (Ed.). *Developing and Evaluating Administrative Leadership.* New Directions for Higher Education, no. 22. San Francisco: Jossey-Bass, 1978.
Hoyt, D. P. "Evaluating Administrators." In R. F. Wilson (Ed.), *Designing Academic Program Reviews.* New Directions for Higher Education, no. 37. San Francisco: Jossey-Bass, 1982.
Nordvall, R. C. *Evaluation and Development of Administrators.* AAHE-ERIC/Higher Education Research Report No. 6. Washington, D.C.: ERIC Clearinghouse on Higher Education, 1979.

Evaluation of Programs

Anderson, S. B., and Ball, S. *The Profession and Practice of Program Evaluation.* San Francisco: Jossey-Bass, 1982.
Craven, E. (Ed.). *Academic Program Evaluation.* New Directions for Institutional Research, no. 27. San Francisco: Jossey-Bass, 1980.
Feasley, C. E. *Program Evaluation.* AAHE-ERIC/Higher Education Research Report No. 2. Washington, D.C.: ERIC Clearinghouse on Higher Education, 1980.
Marcus, L. R., Leone, A. O., and Goldberg, E. D. *The Path to Excellence: Quality Assurance in Higher Education.* ASHE-ERIC/Higher Education Research Report No. 1. Washington, D.C.: ERIC Clearinghouse on Higher Education, 1983.

Evaluation of Research

Baugher, D. (Ed.). *Measuring Effectiveness.* New Directions for Program Evaluation, no. 11. San Francisco: Jossey-Bass, 1981.
Rentz, C. C., and Rentz, R. R. (Eds.). *Evaluating Federally Sponsored Programs.* New Directions for Program Evaluation, no. 2. San Francisco: Jossey-Bass, 1978.

Robert A. Scott is director of academic affairs for the Indiana Commission for Higher Education.

Quality is the coin of the realm in higher education, but few colleges or universities plan for it by making use of what could be a uniquely suited instrument for improving quality—the institutional self-study.

Enhancing Campus Quality Through Self-Study

Robert H. Chambers

Quality... you know what it is, yet you don't know what it is.... But some things are better than others, that is, they have more quality. But when you try to say what the quality is, apart from the things that have it, it all goes poof! There's nothing to talk about. But if you can't say what Quality is, how do you know what it is, or how do you know that it even exists? If no one knows what it is, then for all practical purposes it doesn't exist at all. But for all practical purposes it really does exist.... Why else would people pay fortunes for some things and throw others in the trash pile?
(Pirsig, 1974, pp. 184-185).

No matter how hard it may be to define or to measure, quality had *better* exist or many of us in higher education will soon be out of work. For the colleges and universities of America, quality is the coin of the realm. Those institutions that have quality can readily attract the not-so-small fortunes constantly needed to sustain it. But those lacking it risk impoverishment and being tossed on a refuse dump of steadily increasing size. It is small wonder, therefore, that in these economically troubled times the ghosts of Darwin and Spencer shadow a host of presidents, provosts, and deans, whispering in their ears discomfiting truths about the academic survival of the fittest. Fitness in academia is a matter of quality—perhaps, more importantly, of perceived quality. As one authority puts it (Millard, 1983, p. 33): "A plethora of reports, task forces, committees, and commissions in the last few years have identified quality as the major concern in higher education for this decade."

Quality: What Is It?

But what is quality? To answer the question definitively would require a Rosetta stone that administrators and faculty have not yet unearthed. We, like Pirsig's motorcycling Phaedrus, know what quality is and don't know what it is. Although confounded by the paradox that our "major concern" somehow eludes the confinement our scholarly tools for defining and measuring seem to require, we nevertheless believe we know it when we see it. According to Enarson (1983, p. 8), quality is something we know "in our bones." And this we know, too—we cannot survive without it. Consequently, we persist tirelessly in our efforts to depict it as the very mortar cementing the ivied bricks of the institutions we represent. To prove that our claims to high quality are just, we point to the system of peer review and accreditation established to legitimize what we do. The core of that system—and thus a key to academic quality—is the institutional self-study. It is, in fact, our nearest approximation to the Rosetta stone we lack.

Regional Accreditation

The institutional self-study is the centerpiece of the regional accreditation process, which is itself one of three major forms of external review gauged to assess and certify academic quality; the others are professional society accreditation and state agency evaluation. Regional accrediting commissions—of which there are nine recognized by the Council on Postsecondary Accreditation—are organizations composed of the schools in a region that have achieved and maintained accreditation. These commissions' focus is on the institution as a whole, and so they scrutinize not only educational programs but also other areas, such as student services, financial health, and administrative strength (Millard, 1983, p. 34). Such scrutiny as these regional groups can give, however, is necessarily quite limited. Their concern is primarily with the ability of a total institution to meet a common standard that is both minimal and relative. Thus their search, as one observer of the process correctly notes (Scott, 1980–81, p. 21), is for "the lowest common denominator."

No Determiner of Quality. It is clear, therefore, that the establishment of a college's or university's quality cannot rest in the arms of regional evaluators. "Accreditation itself," according to Millard, "does not determine institutional or program quality. It may assess it. It may help enhance it. But educational quality is a characteristic of institutions or programs, not of accrediting associations" (1983, p. 33). What accreditation does is testify that an institution knows what it wants to do, knows how to go about doing it, is in fact already doing what it says it is, and can be expected to continue to do so in the foreseeable future. Fulfilling the institution's tasks—that is, determining its quality—is the collective responsibility of the trustees, administrators, faculty members, support staff, and students who jointly guide its fortunes.

Many Constituencies. The accreditation process exists for a number of reasons and speaks with authority to a host of constituencies both within and beyond the campus gates. Certification by a regional commission is *the* essential imprimatur demanded by the many publics who might be persuaded to support an institution with their presence, their pledges, or their purses. Without that seal of approval, no matter how minimal its substance, prospective students and their wary parents, as well as private funding agencies, government representatives, corporate officers, potential faculty appointees, and even disgruntled alumni, are quite likely to take their patronage elsewhere. With the seal comes the needed assurance that a college or university is qualitatively sound and thus deserving of public confidence and financial assistance. Accreditation, in short, is a matter of institutional life or death.

National Import. In the broader national context, accreditation symbolizes America's unique commitment to democratic higher education. As the academic community's chief means of self-regulation, the evaluation process directed by the nationwide network of regional commissions is intended to demonstrate that freedom and quality go hand-in-hand in higher education and that peer review is essential in maintaining both. It is, however, a demonstration increasingly under siege. Fiscal uncertainty, shaky enrollments, mounting public skepticism regarding academic standards, and escalating bureaucratic demands for accountability are combining to challenge the credibility and integrity of the higher education community (Millard, 1983, p. 36). Thus far, the assault has been contained, but the pressures against self-regulation within academia are steadily rising. Whether they can continue to be effectively sandbagged or not will depend on the ability of the schools and the regional commissions to show that the fundamental principle of peer review remains worthy of public trust. Without that principle, the nature of American higher education would be irredeemably altered. The next few years, as Millard (1983, p. 36) darkly notes, are likely to determine whether regulatory responsibility "continues to rest with the academic community and its accrediting associations or passes by default to other agencies, including the state and federal government."

Minimizing government control of higher education is in the national best interest, and the surest path to keeping federal and state regulators at bay is to cleanse the accreditation process of its recognized impurities. Since the concept of peer review is the heart of that process, the burden is on the regional commissions to show that their evaluating teams, like Caesar's wife, are beyond reproach. An even greater burden, though, rests on the individual colleges and universities, for, as we have seen, that is where the chief responsibility for maintaining academic quality must finally reside. Although from the perspective of the single school the larger national interest will perhaps inevitably be overshadowed by local concerns, the combined impact of hundreds of institutions approaching their accreditation reviews with thoroughness and candor will substantiate the integrity of the process as a whole.

The Institutional Self-Study

As an individual school approaches its particular task, therefore, the major value of the accreditation process is in serving as an incentive for the institution's continuing improvement. In preparing its self-study for the regional evaluation that occurs each decade, the college or university is obliged to step back and look at itself from bottom-to-top in ways it seldom finds the time or the inclination to do in the normal course of events. Far from being a pointless hardship, as some schools seem to view it, this obligation is in reality a rare opportunity to seize and exploit for all it is worth. The chance to raise institutional sights to new qualitative levels does not occur often. The mandate to prepare a searching self-study offers precisely such a chance, and it is one not to be missed. Indeed, the spirit in which a school grasps the opportunity is itself no small indicator of the institution's true quality.

Not for the Regional Agency. To view the accreditation process—and particularly preparation of the self-study—as being somehow chiefly for the benefit of the regional agency and its visiting team is, therefore, a serious mistake. Although the process does meet a variety of needs, it must serve primarily to enhance the institution's quality if it is to continue to enjoy—and deserve—public support. Administrators, trustees, and faculty who fail to understand this critical point both misserve their schools and betray a national interest.

To piece together a proper self-study is *not* to attempt to please outside evaluators by striving to guess what they might hope to discover about the institution. Rather, it is to peer candidly and searchingly at the institution's mission and goals, its resources, its performance, and its future prospects. While such a scrutiny can entail risks and be quite painful, honest self-appraisal is the only true path to high quality. To try simply to gratify the evaluators is to pursue a course of mediocrity. Worse, it is to invite misleading falsification of institutional facts and to hazard demeaning coverup of reality. Such is the route neither to institutional betterment nor to increased quality in the system of higher education in its entirety.

Candor, Integrity, and Quality. The future of the individual schools and of the national network of which they are part hinges on the integrity of both. In the end, the system that sets the standards can be no stronger than the honesty of its singular components will allow. Deception in the assessment of quality serves neither, and, since the self-study is the centerpiece of the accreditation system, it is to its preparation that any proper evaluation of the process must inevitably attend. In such preparation, the candor of a self-study report is a reflection of an institution's integrity (Marcus, Leone, and Goldberg, 1983, p. 18) as well as of its quality, for, in the end, the two are inseparable.

Integrity is the key to a school's ability to profit from its evaluation of its total program; it is what transforms the writing of the self-study from an ordeal into an agent of change by demanding that the institution examine itself honestly and look to its future self-critically. The degree of integrity the college or university brings to this challenge determines just what it is to make of the occasion presented by the accreditation process. Full openness to it allows the grasping of opportunities that all too rarely present themselves: to change for the better; to clarify the institution's identity — its "distinctiveness," to employ the familiar term of sociologist Burton Clark; to diagnose the healthiness of the balance between its goals and its programs, its aspirations and its resources, its romantic dreaming and its realistic prospects.

Assessing Effectiveness. The overall purpose of the process is to assess the effectiveness of the institution as a whole — to measure its quality insofar as it can be measured. An honest assessment requires frank consideration of the objectives a school has set for itself and weighing of the evidence that the school is or is not achieving those objectives. While the unsettling questions often raised by such weighing may escape the comforting precision of quantitative answers, they must nevertheless be tackled if the process is to be meaningful. In some sense, in fact, the process is itself the answer to many of the questions it raises, for if administrators, trustees, faculty, and staff conduct their analyses with intregity, institutional morale can be enhanced significantly even as the public is assured of the school's level of performance and as areas found wanting receive needed attention.

One of the justified charges often leveled at the accreditation process is that evaluation is not a "healthy science, operating from a base of well-established theory and methodology, and with obvious benefits for all" (Fincher, 1973, p. 8). But if the assessment of institutional quality is not strictly scientific or readily subject to quantitative measurement, it can certainly be handled systematically — indeed, it *must* be if the process is to lead to significant institutional improvement. Far too frequently, however, all involved — from visiting team members to on-campus personnel — flounder about haphazardly, lost without the kind of orienting system that guides them in their dealings with their own disciplines. One means of curing this common ailment and thereby ensuring that the accreditation process matters is to treat institutional evaluation as the very essence of education itself (Dressel, 1976, p. 9).

Evaluation as Education. Critical evaluation is, in fact, our reason for being; it is what we in higher education *do*. Thus there is no reason why the searching and systematic standards we bring to our teaching and scholarship should not be brought to the assessment of our institutions' quality as well. To approach the self-study in this way is to make the foreign familiar. It is also to encourage scholarly objectivity to temper any defensiveness that might naturally arise when the quality of one's own school is being judged.

The process of self-regulation and peer review, in brief, must be solidly professional if it is to deserve continued public support. Proof of a college's or university's professionalism is indicated in the quality of its self-study—that is, in the quality of its assessment of its own quality. To state the matter baldly, a school that fails to approach its self-study objectively, critically, and professionally is, in all likelihood, a school lacking in integrity and short on quality. An institution of integrity is one that studies itself systematically, with an unblinking eye cocked simultaneously on enhancing its own quality and increasing its stature within the wider educational community. The institution of integrity, in short, is often also ambitious, interested—perhaps more than it will admit—in making its steady way upward through the generally recognized pecking order of schools of its type.

Representatives of such an institution realize full well that the worthiness of its self-assessment—and thus of that assessment's value to upward mobility—rides uneasily on their ability to keep their critical sights clear as they go about their task. And that ability, in turn, resides in their talent for keeping certain fundamental questions uppermost in their minds even as mountains of data rise around them. Despite the monumental accumulation of material that self-studies invariably generate, the number of these basic questions is actually quite small. The Middle States Association of Colleges and Schools, for example (Middle States Association of Colleges and Schools, 1982, p. 10), suggests that there are essentially only four:

1. Has the institution clearly defined appropriate goals?
2. Does it have the programs and other resources to attain those goals?
3. Does it offer an environment conducive to their attainment?
4. How well does it achieve them?

To these should be added at least one additional question:

5. What steps are to be taken in attaining any reasonable goals yet unreached?

While a self-study might also address countless other questions, these are the ones that matter most. In a comprehensive self-study—the type that most institutions undergo when satisfying regional accrediting agency demands—an institution can provide the necessary focus to keep the study orderly, logical, and coherent. Without such focus, the study can degenerate with surprising ease into mere piles of separate committee reports, a morass of words and charts destined to have slight impact on the institution's future. This, in fact, can be the unhappy result of a self-study prepared primarily for the regional evaluators. Such a study, conducted more for external than for internal purposes, can do little to advance the institution's cause.

Although, as Semrow (1977, p. 4) notes, it is the exceptional self-study that is truly evaluative, the school of integrity wishing to use the accreditation process to enhance its quality must face up to the "big" questions honestly and self-critically, placing its own interests ahead of those of the visiting team. This, of course, is not simply to be self-serving, for in the end the interests of all concerned parties are the same: increasing the institution's quality and, by extension, the quality of the American system of higher education as a whole. Thus, the college or university bent on bettering its programs should celebrate the opportunity to approach the questions with candor, making them the heart of its self-study and, just as important, using the knowledge attained in wrestling with them as a basis for ongoing self-renewal.

Continuous Self-Evaluation. Ideally, the self-study process should be dynamic, with a self-study under way continuously and not just initiated every ten years at the behest of an outside agency. As Kells (1980, p. xi) observes, however, "most self-study processes remain as burdensome, descriptive, mechanical efforts largely unrelated to both the real problems and to the major successes and opportunities of the institution in question." This is lamentable, for to launch a continuous agenda of self-study—while strenuous, to be sure—would be to make permanent the opportunity that the accreditation process presents only periodically. It would be to institutionalize the major questions regarding mission, resources, campus environment, and present and future achievement, thereby ensuring that the motivation for the enhancement of quality remains constant. To keep these questions always to the fore would be to enable the college or university continuously to view itself as a whole, as an institution sure of its integrity and not merely as a collection of self-contained units. It would be to oblige the school to respond each year, and not just each decade, to the "so what?" question—in effect, to justify its own existence to all of its constituencies. In the long run, the heroic efforts required to make self-study continuous, no matter how strenuous, would yield large dividends. For the institution with sufficient stamina and ambition, the high price in energy and psychic expenditure might be well worth paying.

Because of the costs involved and the ever-present press of business as usual, few schools seriously consider continuous, systematic self-study. All too many, in fact, look upon the accreditation process basically as an ordeal to be survived, hardly as an opportunity to be made permanent. After the visiting team's departure, such schools are far more likely to shelve their studies for another decade than to update them regularly. Yet most academic institutions, in their individual ways, do persist in striving for higher quality, including those unwilling to confess to the need for improvement or to look upon the self-study as an effective means of attaining it. The latter should reconsider their positions, for, as noted above, a key indicator of genuine academic quality is precisely an institution's ability to admit that it *can* be improved, its ability to handle the accreditation process objectively rather than defensively. Such an institution, with credibility and integrity already in ample supply, is very likely to emerge from a candid scrutiny of itself even stronger and more securely in charge of its own destiny than before.

Principal Institutional Components. Starting from a position of strength—its confidence in its present worth and its future potential—the college or university determined to improve its quality will face the five major questions without blinking. As it does so, it will employ them as contexts within which to assess each and all of its principal component areas. The number of such areas, of course, will vary from campus to campus, and authorities on the subject differ in their listings as well. While, for example, Scott (1981, p. 3) speaks of the twelve "primary forms of service" to be evaluated when academic quality is being weighed, the National Association of Public Affairs and Administration lists nine areas to be included in an institutional self-study (Marcus, Leone, and Goldberg, 1983, pp. 44-45) and the Middle States Association of Colleges and Schools (1982, pp. 5-27) lists thirteen. What is most noteworthy about such catalogues, however, is not the differences between them but their similarities. They show that all schools, whatever their respective claims to "uniqueness," have in common certain spheres that are essential to all. The Middle States listing, therefore, can be viewed as representative. It includes:

1. The institution's mission, goals, and objectives;
2. Its program and curricula for fulfilling these;
3. The "outcomes" it achieves (its current effectiveness) and hopes to achieve (its aspirations);
4. Its admissions policies, efforts, and results;
5. The services it provides its students once they are on campus;
6. The role of its faculty in serving a school's stated mission and meeting its students' needs;
7. Its administrative organization for facilitating teaching and learning;
8. The role of its governing board (trustees) in ensuring that the announced mission and goals are being fulfilled;
9. Its planning, budgeting, and accounting policies and practices;
10. Its library and other learning resources, including computing's role in meeting the published objectives;
11. The adequacy of its plant and equipment;
12. Its catalogues, other publications, and general public relations posture;
13. Its openness to innovation, experimentation, and future growth.

It is obvious that each of these areas can be easily divided into a myriad of subgroupings, but for organizational purposes the college or university conducting a self-study is wise to focus primarily on a manageable number of critical spheres. Since self-study preparation is quite properly the work of a host of hands, organization can become a major problem if the project's steering committee is lax and undisciplined. A self-study out of control can be symptomatic of impending institutional calamity, for its confusion and disarray may well indicate that potentially fatal illness is festering deep within the school itself. But even if survival is not at issue—and it rarely is in accreditation reviews—a mishandling or badly organized self-study might still have a decidedly deleterious effect on how the college or university is perceived by its own constituencies, by other educators, and by the public at large. Given the increasingly intense competitiveness that characterizes American higher education today, perceived "image" can hardly be ignored by any school, regardless of its actual strength.

Leadership. Thus the accreditation process in general and preparation of the self-study in particular must be approached most seriously by the entire institution under review, not just by those few threatened with extinction or those with lofty aspirations. No matter how uninspired a school may be upon entering self-examination, the stakes are sufficiently high to demand its best effort. In truth, however, "self-study," as Kells (1980, p. xi) notes "has not been seen as a central process of improvement and change in most American institutions" because few college or university personnel initially recognize the review process for the remarkable opportunity it is; the spectre of endless committee meetings and immense amounts of paperwork can easily overwhelm whatever positive impulses they might otherwise be prepared to bring to their joint task. Consequently, what is required if the opportunity is to be fully exploited is administrative leadership equal to the occasion.

Such leadership, if it is to succeed in this situation, must be ambitious, visionary, and articulate. It must be eager to advance the institution's cause, able to see the self-study as a means to this end, and persuasive enough to motivate others to join wholeheartedly in its pursuit. Direction of this stripe normally can come only from a president who enjoys strong faculty support, or perhaps from a particularly able chief academic officer. Only infrequently will an amply gifted faculty member rise to the bait. But whoever is to lead must be capable, in the midst of the ensuing chaos of committee work, of keeping the priorities of the preparation process in order. The best means of doing this is to maintain a clear-eyed focus on the most important question the self-study can raise: Has the institution clearly defined appropriate goals?

Clarity of Mission. First among the five major questions to be confronted in an evaluation, the matter of institutional mission *must* be cleanly fielded if any of the other questions is to be satisfactorily handled. Of the "big" issues to be faced in the review process, it is the biggest of all. As Millard (1983, p. 35) puts it, "The crucial question for accreditation is not how one institution or program compares with another but how effectively the institution or program meets its own educational objectives." If those objectives are not clearly stated, there can be no adequate self-study. A school unable to articulate its own mission has no true identity and thus no genuine "self" to examine. As a consequence, it can have relatively little notion of what it really is doing as an academic institution and only a blurred sense of its legitimate role in the larger educational enterprise of the nation.

A school's high road to academic quality, then, must lead from a clear comprehension of its proper mission and role to identification and design of specific programs and policies required to carry these out. The same priority naturally applies in the preparation of a self-study. As Caruthers (1980, p. 83) observes: "When an institution's mission is well established and understood, it creates a frame of reference for assessing program quality." Thus clarification of mission makes possible both the rational development and the sensible evaluation of academic programs. In the bargain, it serves as potent confirmation of a college's or university's identity, too, for the school that knows its mission knows itself as well.

Mission and Student Satisfaction. It is worth underscoring in this context that clarity of institutional purpose is also directly linked to student satisfaction with the educational experience. According to Kuh (1981, p. 12): "Institutions with numerous missions and purposes send messages to students and faculty that tend to distort the sense of community considered important for a 'developmentally powerful' [the term is Chickering's] experience." Thus, "the degree to which institutions are able to articulate their purposes is thought to be related to a more informed selection process." Since students wish to choose a school whose mission parallels their own ambitions (and those of their parents!), a proper match works to the benefit of everyone. In such a marriage, as Kuh has it, "students are more satisfied with their experiences, are able to work harder with greater satisfaction toward their goals (that by definition are consistent with the institution's goals), and remain in school until they attain their educational aspirations."

As this example implies, clarity of mission is closely related to every sphere and phase of an institution's life, from admission to zoology. Therefore, once it is established and understood—and *only* then—the remaining major questions regarding programs and resources, academic environment, effectiveness of achievement, and future ambitions can be dealt with sensibly. And so can the dozen or so component areas upon which the self-study might focus.

Comprehensive or Topical Self-Study? To be sure, not all of these areas can be, or need be, examined in the same detail in any single institutional appraisal. While a comprehensive self-study is usually in the best interest of virtually every college or university—especially if a decade has gone by since one has been conducted—a school confident of its basic health may choose to give special emphasis to selected areas or issues of particular concern, as Yale did in its most recent review in 1979. When accreditability can be verified through readily available information, such intensive study of selected functions might be more profitable to an institution than a sweeping evaluation touching every program (Middle States Association of Colleges and Schools, 1981, p. 9). Because of its narrowed focus, however, a topical self-study should be undertaken only if a school is conspicuous in its strengths, if its administrative and faculty leaders have given searching consideration to the limitations of such a study as well as to its likely benefits, and, above all, if the institutional mission is clearly and well understood by each of its constituencies. Serious doubts on any of these fronts should lead to a comprehensive assessment.

Whether an institution chooses to undertake a topical or a comprehensive self-study, of course, depends on what it *really* wants to get out of the process and why. The answers to these questions will reveal how seriously the institution wishes to treat the entire review: as a mere exercise to be endured or as an opportunity for careful examination and dramatic improvement. A laggardly or unambitious institution typically will aim its sights low, hoping only to have its accreditation confirmed so that it can return to its everyday routines. In contrast, the institution with high aspirations will seize upon the review as a fine chance to better itself—the route chosen in 1979 by a former women's college in the Northwest which not long before had made the identity-wrenching decision to admit male students for the first time. It will scrutinize its evolving mission with an eye toward sharpening it and then candidly weigh the merits of some or all of its component areas in the balance of that mission. Depending on the school, some of these areas will seem more important and thus receive more attention than others. Yet, in the end, the health of each will prove to be almost equally vital to an institution's future.

Attention to the Faculty. Although there may be little value in ranking the component areas in terms of their presumed significance, it is nevertheless true that, to recall Orwell, some are "more equal" than others. Therefore, just as a school under review must attend to the matter of clarity of mission, so must it also pay heed to its faculty. Without necessarily proclaiming that "the faculty *are* the University" (as a Columbia professor is said to have announced to an incredulous General Eisenhower upon his assumption of the institution's presidency), responsible academic leaders know full well that no serious university or college appraisal can disregard the achievements and needs of its teaching staff. Faculty quality and institutional quality are so intimately joined that an evaluation of one can hardly be divorced from an evaluation of the other. Thus, an assessment of the meritoriousness, morale, and activities of those who teach, as Dressel (1971, p. 280) observes, is essential to an effective self-study and, hence, to sound judgments regarding program worth. Recognizing this fact, a small liberal arts college in the suburban New York area, which, despite its size, had been suffering rather severe morale-damaging communications problems between faculty and administration, recently chose to confront its difficulties squarely in its self-evaluation and, as a result, has since made significant progress toward restoring a healthy balance to the campus community.

Openness to Innovation. Almost as important as attention to the faculty, however, is careful regard for the institution's openness to innovation, experimentation, and growth. Although this item comes last in the catalogue of components listed previously, it nonetheless joins mission clarity and faculty quality at the top of the heap of requisite review topics. It is, in fact, directly tied to both, for without mission support and faculty ambition institutional aspiration is merely a pipe dream. An eagerness to build on strength and to evolve in exciting new directions is indicative of a school's vitality and corporate imagination. It reflects a dynamic sense of purpose, implies a positive faculty aggressiveness, and reveals a confidence that comes from institutional maturity—a willingness to take chances born of a hunger to be at or near the academic frontier. A college or university characterized by such zeal is one that can face the future secure in the knowledge that it will, to recall Faulkner, "not only endure, but also prevail." It can do so because its energy and power will attract— and continue to attract—able students and faculty whose personal aims match its own. They will readily join such an institution in its steady climb up the educational ladder, for they will recognize in its energetic drive many sure signs of high quality. Such signs spell the difference between excellence and mediocrity in higher education.

The Steering Committee's Role. Since a frank and eager self-study is another certain sign of high quality, leaders of a zealous school under review will take care to ensure, insofar as possible, that their own institutional assessment points to loftier rungs on the academic ladder. A substantial step toward this goal is constitution of a proficient and dependable steering committee to preside over the study's preparation. Since, as we have seen, self-examination is hardly an exact science, no precise formula exists for the creation of an ideal steering committee. How it is to be comprised will depend, for the most part, on the traditions, policies, and political realities of the institution. Yet there are sensible guidelines for its formation that a wise college or university will wish to follow.

Since the steering committee will be responsible for establishing the self-study's general structure and timetable, for appointing and guiding work groups to carry out a number of vital topical assignments, for critically examining the reports that these groups provide, and for editing the self-study document that is ultimately produced, its personnel must be creditable campus figures of proven ability (Middle States Association of Colleges and Schools, 1981, pp. 12-14). They must be smart, well organized, politic, and tough. And they must, above all, be able to lead their colleagues through a process that is a veritable mine field of disasters waiting to happen. Like the director of a complex film, the steering committee alone will be able to see the big picture, to view the growing study as a whole, as an entity whose coherence and integrity matter greatly to the institution. If it is to accomplish what is demanded of it, the committee should be small to enhance its efficiency, but it should also be representative of the total institution to enhance its credibility. Evaluation, after all, is a threatening process, especially if candor is to be one of its hallmarks. As Dressel (1976, p. 5) observes, "evaluation done with or for those involved in a program is psychologically more acceptable than evaluation done to them." Thus, it is simply common sense to include in the process those most likely to be directly affected by it. If the steering committee fails in its task for any reason—lack of credibility, inefficiency, disorganization, or timidity—the self-study also will fail. Its proper constitution, therefore, is a necessity.

Assessing the Assessment. Throughout the review, a strong steering committee, acting for the institution as a whole, will continuously monitor the developing self-evaluation. Since a high-quality study is the mark of a high-quality school, a good committee, in short, will be relentless in assessing the assessment. In doing so, it will persistently keep in focus five questions that are, in part, variations of those the study itself should make paramount in evaluating the institution:

1. Does the study show the school to be living up to its declared purposes as outlined in its published statement of mission, goals, and objectives?
2. Is the study honest, objective, and self-critical?
3. Does it positively exploit the opportunity the accreditation process offers by concentrating inwardly rather than outwardly? That is, does it demonstrate that the intent of the process is to improve the institution rather than to pacify the outside evaluators?
4. Does it aim to enhance the institution's "distinctiveness" even while working to maintain its programmatic balance?
5. Does it look to ongoing self-renewal as a permanent aspect of the school's corporate life?

Each of these questions must be answered affirmatively if the institution is to be genuinely enriched by its self-examination, for each question speaks either directly or indirectly to the examination's truest purpose: to serve as an agent for planning and decision making. A worthy self-study does not merely record what a college or university *is* but also acts in whole and in part as a dynamic plan for what a campus can *become* (Kells, 1980, p. 14). The study, in sum, ought to be a loose-leaf working paper for campus planning to enhance quality, not a fixed document bound for the school vaults. Along with presenting all-important evidence of current institutional quality and integrity, it should also function as a powerful evolutionary instrument pointing the way to dramatic institutional change for the better. Given the glacial pace at which most faculties move, it may be the only *real* such instrument available.

References

Caruthers, J. K. "Relating Role and Mission to Program Review." In *Postsecondary Education Program Review: Report of a WICHE-NCHEMS Workshop and Study.* Boulder, Colo.: Western Interstate Commission for Higher Education, 1980.

Chickering, A. W., and Havighurst, R. J. "The Life Cycle." In A. W. Chickering and Associates (Eds.), *The Modern American College: Responding to the New Realities of Diverse Students and a Changing Society.* San Francisco: Jossey-Bass, 1981.

Clark, B. R. *The Distinctive College: Antioch, Reed, and Swarthmore.* Hawthorne, N.Y.: Aldine, 1970.

Dressel, P. L. "Accreditation and Institutional Self-Study." *North Central Association Quarterly,* 1971, *6,* 277-287.

Dressel, P. L. *Handbook of Academic Evaluation: Assessing Institutional Effectiveness, Student Progress, and Professional Performance for Decision Making in Higher Education.* San Francisco: Jossey-Bass, 1976.

Enarson, H. L. "Quality—Indefinable But Not Unattainable." *Educational Record,* 1983, *64* (1), 7-9.

Fincher, C. "Program Evaluation: Approaches and Procedures." Paper presented at annual forum of the Association for Institutional Research, Vancouver, B.C., May 16, 1973.

Kells, H. R. *Self-Study Processess: A Guide for Postsecondary Institutions.* Washington, D.C.: American Council on Education, 1980.

Kuh, G. D. *Indices of Quality in the Undergraduate Experience.* AAHE-ERIC/Higher Education Research Report No. 4. Washington, D.C.: American Association for Higher Education, 1981.

Marcus, L. R., Leone, A. O., and Goldberg, E. D. *The Path to Excellence: Quality Assurance in Higher Education.* ASHE-ERIC/Higher Education Research Report No. 1. Washington, D.C.: Association for the Study of Higher Education, 1983.

Middle States Association of Colleges and Schools. *Handbook for Institutional Self-Study.* Philadelphia: Middle States Association of Colleges and Schools, 1981.

Middle States Association of Colleges and Schools. *Characteristics of Excellence in Higher Education: Standards for Accreditation.* Philadelphia: Middle States Association of Colleges and Schools, 1982.

Millard, R. M. "The Accrediting Association: Ensuring the Quality of Programs and Institutions." *Change,* 1983, *15* (4), 32-36.

Pirsig, R. M. *Zen and the Art of Motorcycle Maintenance: An Inquiry into Values.* New York: William Morrow, 1974.

Scott, R. A. "Quality: Program Review's Missing Link." *The College Board Review,* 1980-81, *118,* 18-21, 30.

Scott, R. A. "Public Expectations About Quality." Paper presented at meeting of chief academic officers of the American Council on Education, Washington, D.C., October 15, 1981.

Semrow, J. J. *Institutional Assessment and Evaluation for Accreditation.* Topical Paper No. 9. Tucson: University of Arizona, 1977.

Robert H. Chambers has taught at Brown and Yale Universities and currently is dean of the College of Arts and Sciences at Bucknell University. He has served on and chaired a number of Middle States evaluation teams.

Although it is difficult, we can and must assess the quality of student services, for they may be more crucial to the success and stability of our institutions than ever before.

Assessing the Quality of Student Services

Joseph F. Kauffman

Readers of this sourcebook are fully aware of the impending decline in the number of eighteen-year-olds between now and the mid 1990s. The demographic facts are clear and only need interpretation in institution-specific or region-specific terms. Nationally, the composition of the student body is changing as well. There is ample evidence of an impending increase in the proportion of older students, part-time students, women, minorities, and others previously underrepresented in the college and university population. While a small number of institutions will still have relatively selective and competitive admissions, the majority will open their doors ever wider in efforts to serve the changing student clientele.

The final report of the Carnegie Council on Policy Studies in Higher Education (1980, p. 54) described the implications of these changes in the following words: "We expect that students will be more nearly the center of attention on campus during the next twenty years than in the past ten. They will be recruited more actively, admitted more readily, retained more assiduously, counseled more attentively, graded more considerately, financed more adequately, taught more conscientiously, placed in jobs more insistently, and the curriculum will be more tailored to their tastes. . . . They will seldom, if ever, have had it so good on campus."

How will our postsecondary institutions meet the needs of the increasingly diverse student body they admit? What basic student services are they obligated to provide, and how do we tell the difference between the adequate and inadequate or the poor and the excellent? What follows is an attempt to provide some perspective on the evolution of student services in higher education, the relationship of student services to institutional mission and goals, and ways of viewing and assessing the quality of student services and student life.

From Student Personnel to Student Development

There have always been expectations in American colleges and universities that someone would be concerned with student life, student housing, and discipline. Leonard (1956) traces student personnel functions back to the early colonial colleges, when presidents carried the burdens for all such matters. The developments in intelligence and aptitude testing in World War I and the related vocational guidance movement that followed added to the expectations that institutions of higher learning had some obligation beyond the provision of classroom instruction. Out of such expectations came what was to be called the student personnel movement, with its separate staff and functions.

It is generally agreed that the student personnel movement developed during the early twentieth century in part as a protest against German-born intellectualism and also as the result of the findings of the psychology of individual differences. Institutions looked for ways to treat students as individuals and to develop relationships with them that would be more personal. It was in the aftermath of World War II, however, that a student personnel point of view was articulated with a firm linkage to the responsibilities of a democratic society. In a period when we were still reeling from our encounters with the evils of Naziism and the holocaust of that war, the student personnel philosophy expressed as an educational objective the provision of experiences that would develop in students a firm and enlightened belief in democracy.

In 1949, the Committee on Student Personnel Services of the American Council on Education published *The Student Personnel Point of View*. Under the leadership of E. G. Williamson, the committee explained the objectives and the need for student services. That classic statement outlined the rationale for providing effective orientation and counseling, adequate housing and study environments, student health services, a sense of belonging to a community, and so on. Such needs are translated into specific student personnel services to be provided by professional staff and faculty. It should be noted here, however, that the committee held that the major responsibility for the student's personal growth rested with the student. The institution provided opportunities and services, but it was up to the student to make use of such opportunities and services. Thus, colleges and universities were called upon to make provisions for a wide variety of student services in a student personnel context: admissions in an information-providing and counseling mode, records that would be of value to the student as well as to the institution, the services of trained counselors to assist in educational, vocational, and other concerns, health services that were preventative as well as treatment-oriented, remedial services to enable students to remove deficiencies that restrict the achievement of educational goals, student activities that enrich college life and build a sense of community, and so on.

The past two decades have seen the reconceptualization of student personnel services. In the aftermath of the student protests and campus unrest of the late 1960s, and with the ending of the *in loco parentis* role of colleges that came with the new age of majority, developmental psychology became an important conceptual base for student services. Student development became one of the major goals of education, and professional staff in the student services field were urged to think of themselves as student development educators.

There is a rapidly growing body of literature on student development. (One publication that provides an effective orientation to the theories and practices of student development, *Student Development in Higher Education,* is edited by Craemer (1980) and published by the American College Personnel Association.) For purposes of this chapter, suffice it to say that the student development approach to student services is an attempt to apply developmental theory—cognitive as well as psychosocial, person-environment interaction as well as humanistic/existential—and to have such a conceptual foundation apply to the classroom as well as to the campus environment and extracurricular activities.

All of this has left many student services staff members somewhat confused as to their own identity and the future of their profession or what its boundaries may be. For example, the field of developmental and remedial education has grown up separately from student personnel work. What I believe are false arguments over a management orientation versus a student development orientation have been common. There are strains between those with a counseling and psychotherapy orientation and those working in student financial aid and housing services. Student development concepts do not lend themselves to the support services or ancillary role in which most student service professionals find themselves. In a period of steady-state or cutback budgets and planning for decline, no one can be sanguine about any part of higher education. Yet, in my view, quality student services have never been more important to the success of a college or university and its stability.

Basic Student Services

The goals of student services should not be considered separate from institutional goals; such services are not free-standing agencies with unrelated objectives of their own. If one views student needs as human needs without any boundary lines, it becomes impossible to separate institutional responsibilities from community responsibilities. Therefore, I view such services, programs, and staff as integral to the overall institutional mission. There is no way to judge the appropriateness or effectiveness of such services except with reference to institution-wide objectives. All institutions serving undergraduates have a responsibility to provide, in some form, the following basic student services:

1. Adequate information to high school students, counselors, and parents to enable an understanding of admission requirements, educational program opportunities, academic expectations, financial aid availability, and student life.

2. An admissions process that is rational and efficient, serving the needs of the faculty as well as the student clientele. Data on the characteristics of students applying and on those admitted or enrolled should make possible an analysis of the effectiveness of a purposeful admissions program.

3. Registrar and records functions that facilitate efficient student registration, desirable schedules, effective classroom and laboratory utilization, and a student data base for use in analyzing faculty and physical plant resource utilization.

4. An orientation program that effectively inducts new students into the programs, opportunities, regulations, and facilities of the institution.

5. A student financial aid service that brings together in one place all information concerning eligibility for financial aid, including scholarships, grants, loans, and part-time student employment.

6. Housing and food services appropriate to the mission and location of the institution. If residence halls are provided, staff and program should reinforce the educational purposes and goals of the institution. If necessary, a service providing information on off-campus housing deemed suitable for student rental also should be provided.

7. Health services that provide for the care or referral of students with illness and that provide educational programs aimed at preventing illness.

8. Counseling and advising services that relate to student needs for academic, vocational, and career information, as well as limited personal counseling.

9. Career placement services that aid students in becoming aware of requirements for specific jobs and that provide opportunities for qualified students to interview with employer representatives.

10. Services for encouraging and enabling a healthy student life and extracurricular environment through student organizations, student activities, recreation, and the like. The staff for such a function should see itself in an educational and developmental context, encouraging student responsibility, participation, and leadership.

Relationship of Student Services to Institutional Mission

The items just listed are the basic student services which, in some form, all colleges and universities should provide. However, since all student services must relate to the specific mission and programs of an institution, one needs to amend these basic services on a situation by situation basis. It is possible to do this by adding a variety of "special" student services in an ancillary way or by expanding the focus of the basic services in such a way as to accommodate the special needs. One way to illustrate this point is to examine the student services implications of an open admissions program aimed at encouraging nontraditional students to enroll. Such a mission, one would assume, would have the support of the faculty and would be reflected in some manner in the institution's curriculum and requirements. Beyond that, the admissions office would have the responsibility of interpreting the purposes of such an admissions philosophy; special testing, placement, and diagnostic services would have to be provided; remedial and developmental instruction would be necessary in the areas of writing, mathematics, science, and study skills in order for some students to be able to meet the prerequisites of many academic programs; and some group and individual counseling services would have to be provided to meet the wide variety of personal needs that would be expected. An institution could attempt to meet all such needs through the basic student services array, or it might create a new service for special students. Either way, such services would seem to be essential if an institution purposefully moves in a responsible way to enroll significant numbers of such nontraditional students.

Let us pursue this further in order to amplify the connectedness of mission to services. If the institution is enrolling large numbers of adult women students, for example, there may be a need for childcare services and for counseling services related to the needs of returning adult students. If a residential college begins to recruit and enroll significant numbers of commuter students, student life staff need to provide ways to make such students part of the campus community. At the very least, we should be perceptive about and seek to remove the dysfunctional and unnecessary barriers that exist for some students. Often it is only our inertia that is the obstacle. Jacoby and Girrell (1981) estimate that 75 percent of all college students in the nation are commuters, and they feel that the percentage is increasing. They argue for a new commuter student perspective instead of attempts to tinker with traditional concepts of residential students. And they provide a model for improving services and programs for commuter students, which was developed at the University of Maryland.

For almost two decades now, colleges and universities have been engaged in special programs for the recruitment and admission of minority students. There has been a variety of practices and programs, with less evaluation of effectiveness than one would wish. Should there be separate staffs for Black and Hispanic student programs? To what extent should such activities be centralized or integrated? At the very least, should we be able to describe the success or lack of success of such programs in accordance with specific criteria? Although the literature does not reveal very much activity of this nature, there is some indication that such assessment does take place. Smith

(1975), for example, describes how student affairs administrators were dealing with such issues at the University of California at Berkeley some years ago. Also, the 1983 annual conference of the National Association of Student Personnel Administrators (NASPA) devoted one quarter of its program to the exploration of student services issues that stem from the new diversity of students. It is clear that institutions often make program and mission decisions about the student clientele they will serve without giving adequate forethought to the student services that will be expected and needed.

In this regard, one also must be concerned about the admission of large numbers of foreign students to institutions of higher education in the United States. It was not long ago that we read of the evils of recruiters abroad, working on commission and admitting Middle Eastern students to American colleges—often colleges totally inappropriate for the professed needs of such students. The most extreme case was the arrival of some foreign students at Windham College, Vermont, which was closing its doors because of financial problems as students were arriving for the fall term. Marville (1981), herself a foreign student, describes the needs of such students and some of the evils of unethical recruitment. She also suggests some possible solutions—particularly that institutions intending to accept foreign students understand why they want to do so and what resources they will need to make available to help achieve institutional and student goals.

Finally, one should note the increasing presence of handicapped and disabled students in our colleges and universities. Section 504 of the 1973 Vocational Rehabilitation Act requires reasonable accommodations and program accessibility for the handicapped. Most institutions designate someone on the student services staff as the coordinator for handicapped services, but the success of such a person's efforts obviously requires the cooperation of faculty and physical plant staff, as well as that of student services personnel. Olson (1981) describes the ways in which student services may respond to these nontraditional students, not only in order to comply with the law but also in the best tradition of higher education.

Faculty, Curriculum, and Academic Environment

Student services support the overall academic and instructional mission of the institution. Yet we know that effective student services cannot, by themselves, produce desired student development objectives. The attitudes of the faculty toward students and student services, the nature of the curriculum, and the overall institutional environment are all vital to the effective functioning of student services. In this regard, the freshman experience is crucial. It is the time when students are most vulnerable, yet they are also enthusiastic, curious, and willing to work hard. If faculty attitudes communicate an unwillingness to take freshmen seriously, if the institution regards the first year as a form of admissions screening in a sink-or swim context, or if there is no way for the student to make a personal connection with the institution — in class or out — then we have a recipe for failure. There is no way to hold student services staff or programs accountable for such a condition.

Similarly, efforts to build out-of-class learning activities in residence halls and student centers require the cooperation of faculty and academic staff. The president and academic deans must have an interest in the success of such efforts, and faculty must either participate in or demonstrate respect for such efforts. Readers will be familiar with study skills programs and tutoring efforts that failed because they were regarded by faculty as lacking professional staff or being subversive to their course objectives. The point here should be clear: Academic and student services staff must work together, and there must be an institutional commitment to the goals of student services. Otherwise, such services will be regarded as coddling students or, worse, undermining the academic standards of the institution. One test of such attitudes, of course, is to ask faculty members about their awareness of student services and their utilization of or referral of students to such services. Awareness of services and perceptions about the validity of such services obviously have much to do with assessments of quality. If students perceive student services as a natural part of the student development experience, they will be much more likely to make use of such help. Conversely, if the perception is that such services are only for those who can't make it on their own, serious perception problems arise that effect the assessment of quality.

Defining Quality in Student Services

As explained earlier in this chapter, quality in student services must be defined in situational or contextual terms. Assessing quality requires that we examine the level of goal attainment appropriate to a particular institution. Therefore, it would not be appropriate to use the same criteria in assessing the student services of Oberlin College in Ohio, a selective, residential four-year college for recent high school graduates, and a non-selective, two-year community college like William Rainey Harper Community College in Chicago. This does not mean that we cannot assess or evaluate quality. It does mean that we have to use criteria and standards appropriate to the mission and goals of individual institutions.

At the outset of this chapter, mention was made of the changing demographic profile in the American population; institutions are facing a declining number of high school graduates; and student retention has become an area of growing concern. Retention is important to budgets and authorized faculty positions. More than just the admissions staff can become interested in developing strategies and programs for improving student retention. Therefore, institutions could set retention goals as well as strategies and evaluate the retention efforts in a variety of ways. A highly selective, private college might examine its admissions criteria and reduce the proportion of high-risk students it admits. It might also evaluate its residential life and counseling services. An open door, public institution might not have any options with regard to admissions, but it could concentrate its resources on improving remedial instruction and tutoring. Further, it could attempt to make the student experience more positive and to find ways of conveying a caring attitude toward its students.

Plough (1979) suggests criteria for judging the quality of student life in colleges and, while all are not suitable for any one institution, most are applicable. Among the criteria he suggests are: high retention, alumni support, good attendance at campus events, absence of intergroup conflict, and low incidence of vandalism and academic dishonesty. He also adds some other criteria that might not ordinarily come to mind: the regularity with which faculty and staff are seen at evening campus events, the availability of awards or rewards for faculty and staff who actively contribute to student life activities, and the ease with which most students could obtain letters of reference from one or two adult members of the academic community.

Harpel (1978) provides a manual for student services administrators concerned with planning, budgeting, and evaluating student affairs programs. The manual emphasizes the importance of having precise definitions of needs for student services and the target populations to be served. Such needs statements help institutions develop reality-based goal statements, and Harpel provides examples of specific goals and objectives for student affairs programs. It is from such statements that criteria may be identified for purposes of assessing quality.

Several other factors deserve attention as well. These include organizational and administrative concerns, staff leadership and morale, and the professional orientation of the student services staff. Is there clearly an organizational structure for student services that provides a chief student affairs leader with access to the president and participation in policy making? Are student services integrated by program and function in such ways that students and their needs are not fragmented? There is nothing wrong with separate, specialized offices and professional staff if they work cooperatively. But if the organizational structure breeds isolation or competitiveness for scarce student services funds, the students are the losers. In addition to departmental and administrative structure, therefore, there should be clear program structures that relate people and resources to program objectives.

The leadership of student services is an important factor in the quality of the enterprise. Someone who is seen as having the confidence of the president should be in charge. That person should be knowledgeable about budgets and the politics of resource allocation. He or she also should be sensitive to staff morale and should be effective in staff and organizational development activities.

In some of the larger institutions, selected student services may be offered in an academic or training mode, rather than in a service mode. For example, a student counseling center may be primarily the extension of an academic department of counseling psychology or social work, in which graduate student interns provide the counseling services under some form of supervision. While the professional counselors care about the quality of the service, their principal obligation may be to the training of their counseling students. The same may be true in other student services as well. While there may be no alternative to such arrangements, they challenge our concepts of purpose and objectives and require adaptation and vigilance. While para-professionals, volunteers, and student interns can perform valuable services, there is some concern about their use in psychotherapy and medical settings. Thus, important issues in setting quality benchmarks would be the qualifications of the persons rendering professional services, the level and intensity of supervision of those who are interns, and, finally, the level of awareness of students seeking assistance as to the credentials of those providing such service.

One final word on this subject is necessary. While understanding the situational and contextual nature of identifying criteria for assessing quality is important, we must have the courage to know what quality is in our setting. If quality is anything determinate, we should know how to distinguish its presence from its absence.

Student Information Systems

Crucial to any assessment of quality in student services is the ability of an institution to retrieve and monitor information about its students. In fact, the first criterion of quality is the extent to which an institution knows what is happening to its students. All institutions have accounting systems that allow analyses of costs for various programs. Today, this is essential for accountability purposes. Similarly, an institution of quality ought to be able to account for the students it enrolls. This means gathering a list of student characteristics at the time of admission in order to develop a freshman profile for use both internally and externally. Beyond the data concerning high school grades, rank in class, and aptitude test scores, there is value in the kinds of data about new students provided by Astin's yearly surveys of college freshmen (Astin and others) concerning freshman values, aspirations, and the like.

In order to plan student services to meet student needs, it is often desirable to understand student perceptions of the learning environment and campus values. A number of instruments exist, published by the Educational Testing Service, that enable institutions to understand the student experience. Such instruments include the Institutional Goals Inventory, a Community College Goals Inventory, and the Institutional Functioning Inventory, all of which measure the perceptions of respondents concerning the ways in which an institution functions. There are a number of instruments for estimating the quality of student living environments, including the College and University Environmental Scales, College Characteristics Index, and University

Residence Environment Scales. Pace has developed a set of measures that enable institutions to measure the quality of student effort. The measures are part of a questionnaire called *College Student Experiences*. The result, Pace (1979, p. 130) indicates, "enables one to analyze the relationships among personal characteristics, college experiences, college environment, quality of effort, and progress toward important outcomes."

Most accreditation self-studies today emphasize outcome or value-added measures that enable an institution to describe what actually happened to the students who graduated. Such measures range from alumni follow-up surveys and placement office data to scores on the Graduate Record Examination and success rates in licensing examinations (nursing, accounting, teaching, and the like). Outcomes studies are extraordinarily difficult to conduct even when the relationship of input to output is known. A highly selective program may have excellent outcome measures, but they may relate more to the input (student quality) than to the impact of an effective program. Nevertheless, outcome measures are important as a way of describing what happens to students. The reader is referred to an outcomes taxonomy and a list of outcome measures produced by the National Center for Higher Education Management Systems (NCHEMS) in 1977 (Lenning, 1977; Lenning and others, 1977).

At the very least, a student information system would also provide information concerning attrition and retention. What happens to students— who drops out (and why), and who transfers (and why)? How long does it take for the average student to complete a degree? What proportion of students receive financial aid and of what type? What student services are utilized by students and with what frequency? What happens to graduates, and what role does the placement office play in obtaining first jobs? Independent colleges have a substantial stake in keeping in touch with former students, for they are potential participants in fund-raising and alumni activities. Public institutions should do likewise.

Finally, a student information system should enable institutional leaders to examine the relationship of its student clientele to its stated mission, goals, and programs. A liberal arts program enrolling more and more students with vocational goals and expectations needs to give attention to its impending difficulties.

Evaluation and Quality

An adequate discussion of evaluation and assessment methodology for measuring the impact or quality of student services programs is beyond the scope of this chapter. Hanson (1978) has edited an entire volume on the subject of evaluating program effectiveness in student services. Readers should be familiar with the array of techniques for needs assessment, goals definition, measures of activity or output, and measures of impact or outcome. There is, obviously, a politics of evaluation that is related to the source of funding. A Title III grant probably will require not only measurable goals but "milestones," with specific deadlines for their achievement. Passing those milestones becomes a part of the evaluation process. There will be some form of assessment built into the accountability system of services funded by state appropriations. Here, measures of activity—numbers of students served or processed—often suffice.

Some student services units have institutional advisory or policy committees composed of faculty, students, and staff; they may be required to make annual reports as well. The advisory committee not only provides the staff with a sounding board for policy decisions but also requires the staff to think about their goals for the service in terms that can be reported back each year for assessment purposes. This may be, and often is, a public relations device to show that important services utilizing institutional resources are being monitored by a representative body. In some cases, key student services are funded primarily by student activity fees, and student government representatives are decision makers on budget advisory committees; the University of California, for example, finances various student services through such fees. Student services staff must convince the students and faculty on such committees of the worth and effectiveness of such services as are supported by these funds. The evaluation techniques are then tailored accordingly.

Perhaps the most common practice for both institutional and program evaluation is the self-study process. Almost all accreditation evaluation begins with the self-study—enabling the institution or program staff to state what it is trying to do and document how well it is doing it. (See Kells, 1980, for a highly recommended guide to the self-study process.) Essential to any self-study are a description of institutional resources made available for specific program purposes, clarifications of the organizational structure and of the persons responsible for carrying out the program, delineation of the qualifications of the staff carrying out the program or providing the services, and a summary of the various kinds of survey data documenting faculty and user perceptions of the worth of the program or service. In fact, serious efforts at surveying student perceptions and experiences and feeding that data back to faculty and staff are key indicators of an attempt to improve quality.

Astin (1982) suggests that one can compare institutions by using a quality measure that reflects the extent to which the institution's educational policies and practices are designed to maximize student learning and development. He would include in such a quality score answers to such questions as:
- Do students regularly evaluate their teachers?
- Do academic advisers regularly receive student feedback?
- Do students regularly provide feedback to administrators on the quality of student services and activities?
- Does the institution attempt to assess how much students actually learn in their courses?

- Does the institution monitor how students spend their time? How much do students study? How much do they interact with each other and with faculty members?

The use of an external evaluator is often helpful in terms of both process and substance. Often an outsider can ask questions that might be resented otherwise; or, because an outsider has no personal stake in the outcome of the process, such an evaluator can get diverse interests to work together in addressing difficult questions. A consultant who is regarded as a knowledgeable professional by the student services staff also has a legitimacy that many internal parties cannot achieve. Many federal grants require the use of external evaluators.

Obviously, it is much easier to measure activity or use of a student service than it is to measure outcomes. Yet the challenge is to attempt to capture some picture of the outcomes, effectiveness, impact, or quality of such a program or service. Dressel (1978), in discussing criteria for evaluation, equates outcomes with benefits. He defines these in student personnel work as follows: "Turning to outcomes, I would suggest that there are five major ones: (1) the general satisfaction or dissatisfaction of the students, faculty, and administration with student personnel work; (2) an increase in retention rates due to better selection of programs and careers; (3) the knowledge and self-understanding generated in those students, faculty, and administrators who are served by the student personnel work program; (4) the development of skills and consequently of improved performance by students served by student personnel programs; (5) the general reputation and the demands placed upon the student personnel work staff. It will be noticed that some of these do not really measure benefits in any direct sense. Satisfaction with a program does not necessarily mean that it is educationally beneficial. On the other hand, dissatisfaction registered by students or faculty probably indicates that the program is, in some way, ineffective, and rather than facilitating the academic program of the campus, is interfering with it" (p. 327).

Finally, in evaluating for quality, one should examine the professionalism and morale of the staff, the physical facilities provided by the institution, the allocation of financial resources for student services, and the level of sensitivity about ethical concerns and adherence to the best ethical practices. Staff professionalism is enhanced by the provision of funds for institutional membership in relevant professional associations—for financial aid officers, housing officers, admissions directors, foreign student advisers, and the like—and for attendance at regional or national meetings of such associations. All such groups also have statements of ethics appropriate to their functions. These codes provide the basis for assessing and guiding institutional practices. Support for such involvement and association with one's professional colleagues is strongly related to the morale of student services staff.

Financial and physical resources are also indicators of the value placed by institutional decision makers on various student services. At present, it is most unusual to find admissions officers in basements or unattractive quarters. But it is not so unusual to find counseling centers in such facilities, often without adequate provision for privacy and confidential meetings with counselors. Just as we examine the adequacy of laboratories and libraries, the physical space and equipment afforded services informs us of their priority and value.

A Final Word

Never before have the needs of our institutions of higher education and the desires of student personnel professionals been more consonant. Our institutions need to attract and retain students who will judge their college experience in the most positive terms. Student services staff have as their goal the production of just such outcomes. There need be no inherent conflict between institutional purpose and student-centeredness.

In recent years, a good deal of concern has been expressed about the future of the student personnel or student development profession. Our colleges and universities will need, more than ever, people who care about the environment in which learning and growth take place, who care about the dreams and aspirations of students, who strive to reinforce the values higher education represents and often falls short of fulfilling. There is no need for the diminution of such work or such workers.

References

Astin, A. W. "Why Not Try Some New Ways of Measuring Quality?" *Educational Record,* Spring 1982, pp. 10-15.
Astin, A. W., and others. *The American Freshman: National Norms for Fall.* Los Angeles: Cooperative Institutional Research Program, University of California at Los Angeles and American Council on Education, annual.
Carnegie Council on Policy Studies in Higher Education. *Three Thousand Futures: The Next Twenty Years for Higher Education.* San Francisco: Jossey-Bass, 1980.
Committee on Student Personnel Services. *The Student Personnel Point of View.* (Rev. ed.) Washington, D.C.: American Council on Education, 1949.
Craemer, D. G. (Ed.). *Student Development in Higher Education: Theories, Practices and Future Directions.* Cincinnati: American College Personnel Association, 1980.
Dressel, P. L. "Measuring the Benefits of Student Personnel Work." In J. Eddy (Ed.), *College Student Personnel, Development, Administrative and Counseling.* Washington, D.C.: University Press of America, 1978.
Hanson, G. R. (Ed.). *Evaluating Program Effectiveness.* New Directions for Student Services, no. 1. San Francisco: Jossey-Bass, 1978.
Harpel, R. L. "Planning, Budgeting, and Evaluation in Student Affairs Programs: A Manual for Administrators." In J. Eddy (Ed.), *College Student Personnel, Development, Administration and Counseling.* Washington, D.C.: University Press of America, 1978.
Jacoby, B., and Girrell, K. W. "A Model for Improving Services and Programs for Commuter Students." *NASPA Journal,* 1981, *18* (3), 36-41.
Kells, H. R. *Self-Study Processes: A Guide for Postsecondary Institutions.* Washington, D.C.: American Council on Education, 1980.

Lenning, O. T. *The Outcomes Structure: An Overview and Procedures for Applying It in Postsecondary Education Institutions.* Boulder, Colo.: National Center for Higher Education Management Systems, 1977.

Lenning, O. T., Lee, Y. S., Micek, S. S., and Service, A. L. *A Structure for the Outcomes of Postsecondary Education.* Boulder, Colo.: National Center for Higher Education Management Systems, 1977.

Leonard, E. A. *Origins of Personnel Services in American Higher Education.* Minneapolis: University of Minnesota Press, 1956.

Marville, A. "A Foreign Student Reports." *College Board Review,* 1981, *120,* 22-26.

Olson, G. S. "Handicapped Student Services: Whose Responsibility?" *NASPA Journal,* 1981, *19* (2), 45-49.

Pace, C. R. *Measuring Outcomes of College: Fifty Years of Findings and Recommendations for the Future.* San Francisco: Jossey-Bass, 1979.

Plough, T. R. "Identifying and Evaluating Major Elements in the Quality of Student Life." *Current Issues in Higher Education,* no. 5. Washington, D.C.: American Association for Higher Education, 1979.

Smith, N. "A Student Affairs Response to the Needs of Special Constituencies." *NASPA Journal,* 1975, *12* (4), 269-274.

Joseph F. Kauffman is professor of educational administration, University of Wisconsin-Madison, and former executive vice-president of the University of Wisconsin System.

Setting objectives and knowing how to evaluate results are particularly important tasks in public relations, because public relations people can easily get caught up in counting news releases rather than assessing whether the target audience has been reached.

Assessing the Performance of the Public Relations Office

Carol P. Halstead

As colleges and universities face a decade of declining enrollments, increasing costs, and a decreasing rate of government support for education, administrators will be forced to take a hard look at each and every function within their institutions to be sure that the quality of performance is high and that each unit is producing cost-effective results. The public relations function is often the first to be scrutinized, not because it doesn't make significant contributions to the mission of the institution, but rather because it is so difficult to measure the impact and results of public relations activities. In the coming decade, that scrutiny will be more intense than ever before. Administrators will need to know how public information activities contribute to the attainment of an institution's goals, whether the institution is getting its money's worth for each expenditure, and whether the overall cost is offset by the office's accomplishments. The real test of a public relations program is its results. Did it pay off at the box office? In alumni clubs? In the development office? In the offices of foundation and corporate sponsors? In the accreditation review? In efforts to recruit high-quality faculty? In attracting grants for new programs, new services, new buildings, the endowment, financial aid?

R. A. Scott (Ed.). *Determining the Effectiveness of Campus Services.* New Directions for Institutional Research, no. 41. San Francisco: Jossey-Bass, March 1984.

Defining the Function

In order to evaluate the quality of the campus public relations function, administrators begin with an understanding of the function and role of the public relations office on college campuses. What is the role of public relations and what does a typical office do? Jacobson (1978b) defines institutional advancement as the management function primarily responsible for maintaining and improving the relationship of an institution of higher education with society and selected publics in a way that most effectively contributes to the achievement of the institution's purposes. The major process by which the institutional advancement function is accomplished is communication, a necessary condition for achievement of understanding and moral and financial support. Inherent in this definition are certain assumptions about the role and function of institutional advancement: (1) It is an institution-wide commitment that seeks to achieve the goals and objectives of the institution and that should be incorporated at the policy level as well as at the operational level of university affairs. (2) It is concerned with the relationships between the institution and its most important publics and thereby with evaluating and interpreting the attitudes, interests, and needs of those publics. (3) Effective communication is the key to achieving support and understanding.

Within institutional advancement, there are a number of functions and responsibilities. Depending on the size of the institution and the commitment of the president and board of trustees to the institutional advancement function, these responsibilities could be assigned to one or more individuals. Among the functions are: public information or information services (including media relations), alumni affairs, community relations, government relations, development (including annual giving, deferred giving, and foundation and corporate relations), publications, research and evaluation, and institutional relations (also referred to as public, external, or university relations).

For the purposes of this chapter, we will exclude the fund-raising function, which is highly specialized and well covered by Jacobson (1978b), and focus instead on assessing the quality of the public relations office. We will also look at its function in the broadest terms, as it seems clear that the role of the public relations office will grow in scope and importance as education faces a downturn in the student market of the 1980s and 1990s. As Philip Kotler, Harold T. Martin Professor of Marketing at Northwestern University's Graduate School of Management and a leader in the field of marketing for nonprofit institutions, says (1977, p. 9), "The best public relations people are becoming increasingly market-oriented and are interested not only in communication but in what is needed and being offered."

An institutional advancement survey conducted by the Council for Advancement and Support of Education gives the first detailed profile of the advancement field (1983). The survey (BanSlyke, 1982a, 1982b) — which covered job responsibilities, organizational structure and reporting relation-

At Carnegie-Mellon University, R. Keith Moore (1981, p. 1), vice-president of university relations, has similar goals but also includes the goal of improving town-gown relations: "To provide a series of well-planned interactions between city, county, and state communities and their leaders so that their rapport is enhanced and the chances are increased that the public sector and the university will both survive."

Goals also can be internally directed—toward increasing the efficiency of the office, improving the quality and design of publications, increasing cost-effectiveness, or promoting better internal communications. For example, John Fairman (1982), director of news services at Western Illinois University, has the goal for 1983-84 of coordinating printed materials and publicity by consolidating the news services and publications offices. Richard P. Allen (1980, p.1), vice-president for college relations at Gettysburg College, "set a 1981-1982 goal of computerizing the records in the college relations division to achieve maximum effectiveness of a new resource." Or, as M. Frederic Volkmann (1982-1983, p. 1) outlined in his 1982-83 goals for Washington University's public relations office, goals can be performance-oriented: "To insure that the university speaks with a clear and consistent voice," for example; and "to develop, market, and assess news and feature material in a way which insures that its full media potential is realized and that it reaches as many constituencies as possible."

Objectives. Objectives should support the broad goals of the public relations office. In evaluating objectives, an administrator should look for statements that are specific, measurable, and achievable. Good objectives setters aim for a destination, not just a means for getting there. Setting objectives and knowing how to evaluate results are particularly important tasks in public relations, as public relations people can easily get caught up in reacting to inquiries, crises, and the needs of other offices or in wallowing in a sea of paperwork and detail. An old story about Elsie the Cow makes the point about results-oriented objectives. The public relations office of the Borden Company put Elsie on display at a fair one summer, and before long 515, 367 people had patted her trademark. The public relations director proudly told the company president, "Think of that! Over 500,000 people at the Texas State Fair, and each of them got a close look at her." "Very nice," said the president. "And then what happened?" (Truitt, 1969, p. 11).

Although many public relations proponents advise against an overemphasis on quantifying objectives, the following questions should be asked when assessing objectives: What is the expected end result? Is there a projected completion date? Is the objective understandable to all? Is it significant in light of the institution's goals?

Each broad goal is likely to be supported by many specific objectives. For example, to achieve the goal of obtaining more recognition for educational research and service programs, Penn State set the following kinds of objectives: to have each writer produce two to three statewide stories per week; to arrange an average of one speaking engagement per day through the speaker's bureau; and to ask one faculty member per month to write an opinion piece for the editorial pages of target newspapers (Ciervo, 1975). In support of Penn State's effort to recruit more black students, the public relations office set several objectives, including improved relations with the *New Pittsburgh Courier* and the *Philadelphia Tribune,* two newspapers that reach Penn State's target market, producing public service ads in support of such events as the black arts festival, and identifying faculty to write opinion pieces, students to feature as scholarship recipients, and graduates to profile (Thies, 1978). Without writing a set of specific objectives to support institutional goals, it is doubtful that the public relations office would have carried out these particular activities. Objectives provide a means for measuring the contributions of the public relations office to institutional goals and for maximizing limited resources in achieving results.

Priorities. Setting priorities for the public relations office is as important as setting goals and objectives. All goals are not equally important; priorities order the institution's goals and determine which activities come first, second, and third. According to the Volkmann survey (1983), only 38 percent of the respondents said they had a set of office priorities. "Without a set of priorities, it's easy for the public relations office to be sidetracked from its basic goals and to jeopardize its productivity," says Volkmann (p. 48), who lists eleven priorities for his institution, Washington University:

1. *National image* — improvement in the national visibility, name recognition, and image of Washington University.

2. *Student recognition* — support for the recruitment and admission of new undergraduate, graduate, and evening students.

3. *National campaign* — assistance with meeting the communications and publications needs of programs supporting the $300 million campaign.

4. *Alumni and development* — support for other alumni and development programs.

5. *Vice-chancellors and deans* — efforts on behalf of the external public relations needs of other vice-chancellors and the deans.

6. *Departments and programs* — furtherance of the other external public relations needs of the departments, institutes, centers, and research programs of the university.

7. *Internal communications* — development of better internal, institution-wide communications that will improve the university's overall self-image and that will, in turn, support a better external public relations program.

8. *Community relations* — maintenance of current local public relations efforts through St. Louis news media, campus events, and publications.

9. *Other external public relations* — encouragement of any other external public relations efforts of Washington University not mentioned previously.

10. *Other internal communications* — help for the internal communications needs of Washington University not mentioned previously.

11. *Other tasks* — performance of any other public relations tasks as may be required from time to time.

Have Audiences Been Identified and Researched?

To be effective, public relations offices must carefully identify the audiences they wish to reach and the actions they want those audiences to take. Target audiences are those groups of people who are in a position to interact with the institution in one way or another: prospective and enrolled students and their parents, donors, legislators, community groups and businesses, alumni, faculty and staff, media, and so on. Key audiences will vary, depending on the goal. Dickinson College, Pennsylvania, for example, cites five audiences to reach in support of student recruitment efforts: prospective students and their parents; high school guidance counselors; high school teachers; information networks (College Board, Barron's, and so forth); and professional peers (Ross, 1982).

Communications with each target audience must focus on the kind of attitudes and behaviors an institution wants each audience to exhibit. "Having a good opinion" of an institution is not a behavior but an attitude. Inquiring about the computer science program or supporting the alumni fund are behaviors an institution wants to encourage. Knowing the attitudes and opinions of target audiences is an important step toward influencing their behavior. Here is where research comes into the picture. A plan that is based on research into attitudes and opinions of key audiences is likely to be much more effective than one that is not. As Edward Meek, director of public relations at the University of Mississippi, says (Skelly and Meek, 1982, p. 19) "Positioning an institution in the marketplace without research is like attempting to parallel park with your car windows fogged up. If you can't see where you are going—or where you have been—you are likely to bounce off a bumper or two and still not wind up where you want to be."

Though the use of market research to assess audience attitudes and opinions is not yet widespread in higher education, there has been a tremendous growth in its application in the last four to five years. In a declining student market, more and more institutions have realized the importance of developing communications programs that acknowledge real information gaps and real opinions held by target audiences. Listening formally and informally to key constituencies will enhance the effectiveness and efficiency of an institution's communications, as well as provide a way of monitoring and evaluating results. The fact that a public relations program includes a market research step is not in itself an indicator of the quality of the program, however. In assessing quality, an adinistrator should look for the following:

1. *A commitment to action.* All too often, studies are conducted but the results sit on the shelf collecting dust. To ensure action, there must be an institution-wide commitment to the effort. Have provisions been made for sharing the findings with key administrators? Is the institution in a position to take action based on the findings? Are there sufficient staff and resources available to implement the results?

2. *Clear and specific identification of needs, objectives, and audiences.* Surveys

that try to research all things for all people usually result in little solid advice for anyone. An effective research program clearly defines what the institution needs to know from which audiences and for what specific purposes. In higher education, there are many reasons for conducting audience attitude and opinion research: to assess the quality and effectiveness of an institution's recruitment literature, to test messages, to determine what appeals are most effective in attracting contributions from potential donors, to understand why students drop out, to evaluate which factors most influence students' decisions to enroll in an institution, to determine how alumni view the institution's plans for a new performing arts center and how likely they are to support it, to explore attitudes and opinions of potential contributors, and so on.

Some of the pioneering work in public relations research in higher education began at the University of Mississippi in 1969 (Skelly and Meek, 1982). Every three to four years, Ole Miss studies attitudes of high school students, enrolled students' parents, high school counselors, community college students and alumni by using direct-mail questionnaires and telephone surveys. As a result, the university has revamped its entire publications program, adopted new themes and slogans to reflect the changing attitudes and interests of students, identified and filled communication gaps, and identified and acted on strengths and weaknesses of the university as a whole.

Chapman College in Pittsburgh set up panels of students from two local high schools to obtain information about the effectiveness of college viewbooks (Parker, 1976). Five groups of students were shown eighteen different college viewbooks with different styles, designs, and formats, and asked why they chose certain viewbooks over others. The result was a total new look at Chapman incorporating the students' preference for no-nonsense text, attractive four-color design, and practical, specific information about programs and costs.

3. *Effective research techniques.* Whatever the research techniques used—mail surveys, telephone interviews, focus groups, or personal in-depth interviews—it is important that the research be done carefully to achieve maximum usable results. Since few public relations officers have training or experience in this field, the assistance of an institution's office of institutional research, department of marketing or sociology, or an outside consultant might be effective in ensuring that issues relating to sample size, pretesting, demographic and psychographic characteristics of the audience, multiple-choice and open-ended questions, reliability, and validity are handled properly.

Have Messages, Slogans, and Themes Been Carefully Developed for Each Key Audience?

One of the major goals of research is to determine what messages or appeals will influence key audiences' opinions and motivate them to take desired action. Such messages are the content of communications, and they are the themes that appear over and over in institutional communications programs. In evaluating a comprehensive public relations program, administrators should look for key statements, themes, and slogans that are likely to generate the opinions and actions the institutions seek.

There are two important kinds of messages: those that focus on benefits to the audience, on "what's in it for them," and those that focus on the strengths and features of the institution and its programs. Different benefit messages should be directed at different audiences, depending on their relationship to the institution and the information needs and interests of the audience.

A recent survey by the Council of Independent Colleges (CIC Public Information Inventory, 1982) of the public relations needs and practices of small private liberal arts colleges identified a number of benefits of these types of institutions that would appeal to different audiences. The feature of small size, for example, translates to some parents as a safe and nurturing environment, while for students small size means a chance to participate in many campus activities and to get to know faculty and peers well. For business and government audiences, the benefit of being small is that the institution is responsive and free to innovate. Sample benefit slogans used by small colleges include: "Academic excellence at an affordable price" (Bethel College, North Newton, Kansas), "We give you a chance to grow" (Buena Vista College, Storm Lake, Iowa), and "An environment you can trust" (Anna Maria College, Paxton, Massachusetts).

Unlike benefit messages that put the audience's needs and interests first, messages about features stress the strengths, uniqueness, and advantages of the institution. The Council of Independent Colleges also identified a number of themes that small private colleges are using to promote the features and services of their institutions: Central College of Iowa administers 6 study abroad programs that enroll nearly 3,000 students from more than 600 other American institutions. Briarcliff College is the most affordable coeducational Catholic college in Iowa. Dominican College in New York has a unique program to prepare teachers of the blind. Friends University in Kansas offers a course in the physiology and psychology of fatigue, reported to be the only course of its kind in the nation.

Has a Strategy Been Developed for Reaching Goals and Objectives?

Once reached and developed, messages should be delivered consistently and continuously with the ultimate goals of establishing a position in the marketplace that identifies the institution as being unique, special, or different from other institutions. This process, known in advertising as positioning, is based on the reality of today's overcommunicated society. People can comprehend fully only so many messages that are sent out. The more specific, unique, and repetitive the message, the more likely people are to remember it. For example, in 1977 Appalachian State University in North Carolina began to adopt a strategy of playing up its "boondock" location in the belief that rural and small are better than urban and large (Moore, 1981). The university released a regular "Folk Ways" column, featured pictures of the mountains, and targeted its communications to the typically poor but proud people in the region by concentrating on weekly newspapers and local radio. Carnegie-Mellon University, on the other hand, has recently adopted a strategy of moving from a regional to a national institution by playing up its strengths in computers and robotic technology. To accomplish this, Carnegie-Mellon has made a broad-based, well-planned, aggressive national media relations program its top priority. By establishing itself as a leader in computers and technology, Carnegie-Mellon University hopes to attract high-caliber students, larger amounts of financial support, and a greater number of research contracts for faculty (Moore, 1981).

Have Appropriate Channels of Communication Been Selected to Reach Key Audiences in an Efficient and Effective Manner?

Identifying and selecting means of communicating with an institution's key publics is one of the most important roles of the public relations office—and the one with which it is often most closely identified. Here is where training and experience in the media, communications, journalism, marketing, and the social sciences becomes important. Knowing how to select media at the right time is a function of matching the needs, interests, and characteristics of the target audience, the media, and the institution. Though public relations is often confused with one of its functions—publicity through mass media—administrators should look for a total public relations program that uses both independent media, such as television, radio, newspapers, and magazines, and captive media, such as advertising, direct mail, such internal publications as newsletters and alumni magazines, films, and publications. The public relations office also should use special events, luncheons, conferences, and one-to-one communications.

Personal communication is the most effective means of communication, but it is also the most expensive. In an unpublished manuscript, M. Frederic Volkmann (n.d.) at Washington University lists, in order of importance, commonly used means of communicating an educational public relations message:

1. One-to-one, face-to-face conversation.
2. Small group discussions or meetings generally of five persons or less.
3. Person speaking before a group where questions and dialogue are encouraged.
4. Telephone conversation between two persons.
5. Hand-written, personal letter.

6. Typewritten personal letter that clearly was not generated from a computer data base or typed by an automatic machine.
7. Computer-generated or word-processor generated "personal letter."
8. Mass-produced, nonpersonal letter.
9. Brochure or pamphlet sent out as a direct-mail piece without a covering letter.
10. Newsletters, magazines, tabloids, and so forth developed and distributed by the institution.
11. News carried in newspapers, radio, television, magazines, and so on.
12. Advertising in newspapers, radio, television, magazines, and so on.
13. Other less effective forms of communication (such as billboards, skywriters, and so on).

Most communications programs will, in fact, combine many if not all of these techniques. What is important to look for in evaluating the program is the mix and timing of communications techniques and strategies that are used. For example, the role of the mass media in student recruiting is to create awareness and a positive climate for the institution. Favorable press coverage alone will not convince a student to enroll, but it can generate awareness and interest and attract inquiries, thereby limiting the number of people with whom the institution has to communicate more directly. Direct-mail brochures sent to targeted lists through the College Board's Student Search Service will also generate awareness and interest, but to "make a sale," so to speak, an institution must give prospective students an opportunity to evaluate the institution. Communications at the evaluation stage move up the Volkmann scale and become more and more personalized. Colleges provide numerous ways for the student to "try out" the institution, from viewbooks to student newsletters, college fairs and high school visits, phone calls from admissions counselors, special events on campus, and one-to-one meetings with faculty and advisers.

Knowing what channels and vehicles of persuasion and communication actually set into motion the social processes necessary to influence opinions and behavior is an important skill that takes time, experience, and research.

Does the Program Provide for Monitoring and Evaluation?

Evaluating and reporting the results of public relations efforts is considered by most practitioners to be the most difficult — as well as the most costly — part of the public relations program. Yet if a public relations office is to mount an organized effort to achieve goals, then it is imperative to build into the program steps for monitoring progress and evaluating results. In today's atmosphere of declining enrollments, rising costs, and decreasing rates of government support, evaluation is even more critical. In an article in the *Public Relations Quarterly,* Harvey K. Jacobson (1980, p. 7) presents several reasons for evaluating public relations programs: "A good manager should always be considering alternative courses of action, and evaluation helps you to decide which course to take. Evaluation provides feedback about program effort, performance, and effects. This information is valuable in conducting daily operations, controlling current performance, and planning strategically for the future. Evaluation reduces reliance on crisis management."

Successful evaluation requires effective planning and objective setting. For example, it is impossible to measure results of an effort "to build a positive image of the institution," but one *can* measure an effort to help the admissions office recruit more minority students. In looking at evaluation procedures, administrators should answer the following questions: Do evaluation techniques and strategies reflect program goals and objectives? Are the goals and objectives of the evaluation itself clearly stated? With whom are the results to be shared, and are those individuals involved in the evaluation process? Is there commitment from the top, and have sufficient resources been allocated? Is the strategy for evaluating the program appropriate? Can decisions be made on the basis of the final report, and is a system in place for following through and implementing results?

What, then, can be measured and how is it done? The real difficulty in conducting research is knowing when to do what, with whom, and for what purpose. As Jacobson points out, the effect or impact of a public relations program can be measured in terms of contact, response, and relationship with the audience. Most public relations offices that do evaluate their efforts spend most of their time and money on measuring audience coverage—tallying, for example, the number of reporters at a press conference, alumni at a fund-raising event, press clippings, air mentions, film showings, or direct mailings. Administrators should not look only at the volume of mailings, news releases, publications, advertisements, or even clippings to measure effectiveness, however. Dissemination, in other words, does not equal communication. As researcher Charles R. Wright (1955) once pointed out, "Unread leaflets, unheard broadcasts, unviewed films—however abundantly and skillfully produced—have no chance of influencing an audience that is not there. And volume of output does not guarantee that an audience is reached."

A second step in evaluating the reach of public relations is to evaluate the influence process—who's listening to what and with what effect. Monitoring which media are reaching target audiences and how audiences are responding requires systems for counting and tracking inquiries and for surveying constituents to get their reactions. For example, a systematic analysis of which communications vehicles are generating responses (inquiries for applications, for transfer information, money or pledges from fund-raising appeals, and so on) will tell the public relations office the effectiveness of different media outlets. Keeping track of inquiries by using box numbers on data collection sheets may demonstrate, for example, that publicity outpulls advertising or that a publication thought extremely important was actually of little use in generating gifts or students.

Audience surveys can tell an institution even more about its effectiveness. Georgetown University, for example, conducted one of the early audience surveys in 1971 to determine how its radio and television program called "Georgetown University Forum" was received both by stations and by listeners and viewers. A mail survey of stations and a telephone survey of potential listeners in two cities resulted in a decision to discontinue the time-consuming and ineffective television production and to reduce the length and improve the quality of the radio program to meet better the needs and format of the radio stations and the interests of the audience (Ciervo, 1975).

Response and Relationship

Measuring the audience's response (level of understanding, acceptance, support) and the relationship between the institution and the audience over time is more difficult. Attitude surveys, opinion polls, and readership surveys, for example, often require special expertise and large budgets. Methods of evaluation must be consistent with the intent of the communication, whether it is to inform, persuade, reinforce, or move the audience to action. There is a tremendous range of measurement possibilities—from studying attitudes or opinions over time to measuring how well known an institution or specific program is compared to its competitors or the relative importance of factors influencing students' choice of a college. The selection of methods of research will depend on the purpose of the study. Whatever the goals or the methods of evaluation selected, administrators should keep in mind the same guidelines listed earlier in the section on evaluating market research activities.

In the final analysis, educational institutions must be responsive to the publics they serve. At the same time, institutions depend on these same publics for understanding and support. It is in the communications process that the exchange of values between the institution and its most important publics takes place. Administrators who understand the communications process and know how to evaluate the quality of the performance of its public relations office stand a much better chance of making that relationship a productive and successful one for both parties.

References

Allen, R. P. *1980-85 Goals for College Relations Division.* Gettysburg, Pa.: College, Relations Division, Gettysburg College, 1980.
BanSlyke, J. K. "We the People of CASE." *CASE Currents,* 1982a, *8* (6), 26-38.
BanSlyke, J. K. "We the People of CASE." 1982b, *8* (7), 18-22.

CIC Public Information Inventory. Washington, D.C.: Council of Independent Colleges, 1982.
Ciervo, A. "How We Use Research in Public Relations Management." Speech presented at American University institute, Washington, D.C., November 14, 1975.
Ciervo, A. *Public Relations Goals.* State College: Office of Public Information and Relations, Pennsylvania State University, 1981.
Corbitt, T. "Position Your Institution." *CASE Currents,* 1977, *3* (5), 34-35.
Fairman, J. *Mission, Goals, and Objectives.* Macomb: University News Services, Western Illinois University, 1982.
Jacobson, H. K. "Framework for Evaluation: Indicators of Effort, Performance, Effects." In H. K. Jacobson (Ed.), *Evaluating Advancement Programs.* New Directions for Institutional Advancement, no. 1. San Francisco: Jossey-Bass, 1978b.
Jacobson, H. K. "The Evaluation Process: Its Importance to the Manager." *Evaluating Advancement Programs.* New Directions for Institutional Advancement, no. 1. San Francisco: Jossey-Bass, 1978a.
Jacobson, H. K. "Guidelines for Evaluating Public Relations Programs." *Public Relations Quarterly,* 1980, *25* (2), 7-10.
Kotler, P. "Why We Need Marketing." *CASE Currents,* 1977, *3* (5), 4-9.
Moore, R. K. *Strategic Plan.* Pittsburgh, Pa.: Public Relations Division, Carnegie-Mellon University, 1981.
Parker, L. "Why Chapman Opted for a Four-Color Viewbook." *CASE Currents,* 1976, *2* (2), 23-25.
Ross, J. "Goal-Oriented Public Relations Plan." Speech delivered to the Council of Independent Colleges national institute, Washington, D.C., June 1982.
Skelly, G., and Meek, E. "Defog with Research." *CASE Currents,* 1982, *8* (5), 19-23.
Thies, A. H. "Practicing Public Relations by Objectives." *CASE Currents,* 1978, *4* (1), 23-25.
Truitt, R. H. "Wanted: Hard-Headed Objectives." *Public Relations Journal,* 1969.
Volkmann, M. F. "Be Prepared: Plan To Get the Most from Yourself and Your PR Staff." *CASE Currents,* 1983, *9* (6), 48-53.
Volkmann, M. F. *One Year Plan.* St. Louis, Mo.: Public Relations Office, Washington University, 1982-1983.
Volkmann, M. F. "Planning and Organizing the Public Relations Program for Success." Unpublished manuscript, Washington University, St. Louis, n.d.
Wright, C. R. "Evaluation of Mass Media Effectiveness." *UNESCO International Social Science Bulletin,* 1955, *7* (3), 417-430.

Carol P. Halstead is president of College Connections, a firm that specializes in developing public relations and marketing communications programs for educational, health, and other nonprofit institutions and associations and for business associations and firms interested in the educational market.

assumptions about the world in which we live. Qualitatively, in a modern society, cooperation connotes civil exchange, friendship, diplomacy, and compromise—all fundamental to human exchange of the highest quality. A breakdown in cooperation leads to a breakdown in communication and eventually to disorder. Quantitatively, increased cooperation assumes less duplication and, presumably, increased services and reductions in costs. Thus, cooperation is a critical component in a productive environment.

As one embarks upon a cooperative or sharing effort, however, several questions must be considered as part of the planning for the new effort and in anticipation of evaluating it:

1. What does cooperation mean when it assumes sharing? Sharing does not mean an equal contribution of resources from participants; some may give more than others. Cooperation, therefore, requires a sharing of resources, responsibilities, and benefits in a manner that is defined before the cooperative venture is implemented.
2. What are the costs of cooperation and sharing? While partners in a venture may not share equally in bearing costs, they will each bear them, whether they are direct, indirect, or opportunity costs. One of the biggest costs will be in terms of time—time for meetings and planning. These costs, too, must be considered when preparing budgets, reviewing progress, and evaluating the benefits derived from the cooperative venture.
3. What tensions will be created when conflicts occur between local autonomy and cooperative responsibility? Cooperation requires mutual agreement and compromise, a balance between the competing values of local autonomy and cooperative responsibility. The likelihood of tensions arising between them is high. Therefore, the contract or letter of mutual understanding should detail not only agreements concerning the sharing of costs, responsibilities, and benefits, but also procedures for resolving conflicts. Any evaluation of the venture will assess these procedures as well.

Membership in a cooperative effort will have permanent long-range effects on an institution. Therefore, the academic, legal, and economical issues raised by education-industry cooperation—potential conflicts of interest, academic freedom, free exchange of information and questions about patents, exclusive licenses, commingling of funds, as well as royalty rights—provide an important backdrop in the development of planning and evaluation procedures. Because of these problems, which are inherent in any cooperative effort, the process one uses in planning is critical. In fact, in many instances, process becomes more important than product or outcome, because it establishes the tone and nature of relationships that may become permanent. Plans can be changed, but the emotional commitments and trust (or lack of it) are extraordinarilty difficult, if not impossible, to alter if severely damaged.

Planning Assumptions

The basic components of cooperative planning can vary widely. Outlined briefly here are components that are probably essential ingredients of plans for good cooperative efforts.
1. Planning must be a participatory process. When priorities are being established for the use of limited available resources, affected groups should have input into the decision-making process.
2. The need for the participation of different interest groups in planning suggests the use of a decentralized planning procedure. This, in turn, implies that planning may be conducted best when it takes place as close to the grass roots as possible.
3. Assumptions must be clearly established and reasons for the establishment of priorities should be fully explained. Planning assumes a certain value system. Assumptions are made, sometimes explicitly but more often implicitly, as to who should be served and how. Priorities for action are then established and organized according to these assumptions. Assumptions, therefore, must be clearly stated.
4. The role, scope, and functions of an institution must be examined carefully and defined clearly as part of or in relationship to the planning and evaluation process.

Planning Steps

1. Overall goals must be established and clearly articulated. When goals are being determined, the following questions must be addressed: What will be the acceptable scope of the content, quality, and purpose of the organization's efforts? How can the burden of the costs of services be shared and distributed among participants? What will be the time schedule for achieving the accepted goals and how will the process be phased? Is the effort consistent with the institution's mission?

    A set of premises, formulated with as much clarity as possible for each situation, is needed to serve as a set of social parameters. These values affect the characteristics and functions of the system and will determine the focus and relevance of the planning process. When establishing goals, planners should focus on the services the institution performs best. Officials should be cautious about taking on functions the institution is not equipped to handle. They should carefully define the institution's role so that it will furnish only those services that are not currently available — or not available at the level of quality proposed — through other institutions or organizations.
2. Links with industry need to be established and questions addressed:

What industries need technical assistance in areas in which the institution excels? Who are the appropriate persons in the industry to contact? How should the initial contact with an industry be made? What formal communication network is necessary for a long-term working arrangement?
3. Mutual goals and assumptions need to be agreed upon by the cooperating parties: What working assumptions have been made concerning patents, profits, copyrights, faculty consultancies, student involvement and compensation, and so on? What will the arrangement cost? Who will pay? Who should be doing what, where, and when? What are the time frames for implementation and completion?
4. A determination of the fiscal and human resources available for the shared services should be calculated.
5. If demand for services exceeds the resources available for supplying the services, institutional priorities will need to be reevaluated and, if necessary, reestablished.
6. Implement the plan.

Evaluation

The planning procedure must be a *continuous* process with appropriate attention devoted to: The reevaluation of goals; the participation of those affected by and interested in the planning process; the assessment of existing needs and resources; the assessment of new needs; and the methods for meeting those needs (financial, structural, and programmatic). Planning must not be a static process. It should be seen as a continuing process, a framework for adjusting to new needs as they occur while eliminating services no longer in demand. The flexibility needed to respond to a rapidly changing environment should be built into carefully designed planning procedures.

In this regard, planning is evaluation and evaluation is planning. One is inextricably tied to the other, as Van Maanen (1979) illustrates. By placing one circle on top of another so that they share one point, called *assess* (six o'clock on the top circle and twelve o'clock on the bottom), Van Maanen shows visibly how the planning cycle (the top circle) of plan, implement, assess, and decide, coincides with the evaluation cycle (the bottom circle) of assess, specify, measure, and compare. The two cycles become one process of planning objectives and operation, implementation, assessing outcomes and costs, and deciding whether to continue the present operations or develop a new plan (Lehmann, 1981).

Examples of Cooperation

It is important for any institution embarking upon an effort to develop ties with industry to discover what types of activities linking business and education are currently underway. Many types of cooperative efforts are presently in operation, and many more are being planned. Such popular magazines as *Buiness Week, Fortune,* and *U.S. News and World Report,* in addition to such special interest papers as *The Chronicle of Higher Education* and *Higher Education Daily,* offer numerous examples of new business–education liaisons:

Business and Campus Personnel Exchanges. Professors are serving as consultants to both management staffs and research and development teams in industry; businessmen are helping reevaluate curricula, particularly in business education and engineering; and academics are starting new businesses of their own, both on and off the campus (for example, at Kansas Wesleyan College, an assistant professor of computer science runs his own software company from the college department).

Industry-Funded Research and Development. Industries are funding university research centers; such as the Microelectronics Institute at Stanford, the Robotics Center at Carnegie-Mellon, and the Forrestal Center at Princeton. Companies are giving equipment to schools: For example, IBM is offering $50 million in cash and equipment grants to universities wishing to develop or update manufacturing education. Some companies are donating money for more innovative research: Sohio, for example, has a $10 million national campaign to stimulate more innovative research in campus laboratories.

Cooperative efforts of business are resulting in consortia of businesses pooling their resources. The semi-conductor industry has formed Semi-Conductor Research Corporation to funnel corporate research and development funds into universities. Its first award was given to support research on integrated circuits at the University of California at Berkeley, Carnegie-Mellon, and eight other universities. Another example includes Control Data and TRW, which have joined with other companies and Purdue University in a major effort to develop the first factory that will be completely computer-controlled, from product design all the way to the loading dock.

Business and education are involved in joint research with interesting and practical results. For example, students at Worcester Polytechnic Institute, Massachusetts, are designing robotics systems for Emhart Corporation. The collaborative project has already paid dividends on its $1.5 million investment in equipment and management time.

Education-Supported Research and Development. Educational institutions are providing technical support to help new businesses emerge and thrive. Support comes in the form of new ideas, development of prototypes, market studies, and evaluations. Examples include the Center for Entrepreneurial Studies and Development at West Virginia University, Innovative Service at the University of Wisconsin, and the Technology Development Center at the Georgia Institute of Technology.

Consortia of Business/Education/Labor/Finance. Consortia, which include some of the key actors in a community—business, education, labor, and finance—are evolving to encourage and support innovation. In Pennsylvania, the Franklin Partnership, operated by a consortium of colleges and universities, business, labor, and financial institutions, helps establish centers for advanced technology.

Next Steps for the Alliance

These types of activities are just a few examples of the many available opportunities for business and education to work together. Each institution must determine for itself where its talent might best be used. This presentation of examples is meant to reinforce the concept that a partnership can work and that it can be beneficial to both parties if attention is given to the appropriate and necessary planning and evaluation. Forging these new relationships will take time, energy, and dedication to reestablishing excellence in America. Cooperative efforts require more than dollars. They demand a commitment to solving mutual problems and a genuine desire to work toward common goals.

This new alliance of business and education, however, requires the sensitivity of both parties to the different roles education and industry play in American society. As expressed in "Business and University: A New Partnership" (*Business Week,* 1982), this new venture presents problems as well as opportunities. The new partnership raises legitimate concerns to which business should be sensitive. Some educators, for example, worry that placing too much emphasis on commercial objectives could undermine the fundamental task of universities to teach, preserve, and enlarge the broadest possible cultural heritage. This danger can be avoided. Already groups of business executives and educators are meeting to develop guidelines for business-college cooperation. In their own interests, companies should avoid tying their support of university research to specific or short-term commercial payoffs. Corporations are not charitable institutions, of course, but they can amply justify their support for campus research on the basis of broad, long-range benefits.

A second, less obvious potential danger deserves equal attention. In their new-found enthusiasm for supporting technology and the professions, companies should not shortchange the humanities. Great universities are not trade schools; they are the repositories of the culture that help nourish and advance both science and technology. Liberal arts should also receive solid business support.

The possibilities are endless, and the prospects are indeed very exciting. In the last analysis, however, these new ventures will begin when persons of vision make them happen. Forging this new territory requires leadership that will reshape the values of our institutions.

References

"America Rushes to High Tech for Growth." *Business Week,* 1983, *2783,* 84–90.
"Business and University: A New Partnership." *Business Week,* 1982, *2770,* 58–62.

Lehmann, T. "Evaluating Adult Learning and Program Costs." In A. Chickering and Associates (Eds.), *The Modern American College: Responding to the New Realities of Diverse Students and a Changing Society.* San Francisco: Jossey-Bass, 1981.

"The New Economy." *Time,* 1983, *121* (22), 62–70.

O'Brien, P. "Educational Skid Affecting Economy." *St. Paul Pioneer Press,* February 16, 1983, p. 6a.

Susan Powell became manager of research and evaluation for the McGraw-Hill Book Company in May 1983. For the five years prior to that, she was director of program planning and coordination for the Minnesota Higher Education Coordinating Board.

Libraries and computing facilities are important assets for achieving high-quality instruction and research, yet most evaluation of them dwells on inputs, not outputs.

Evaluating the Effectiveness of Academic Libraries and Computing Facilities

Donald R. Brown
Shirley M. Smith
Robert A. Scott

Libraries and computer-based information activities soon will merge into campus "information utilities." In fact, many universities are already in the first stages of this synthesis. Because these campus hybrids will require administrators to plan future budget allocations and organizational structures with few road maps in hand, it is important now to evaluate the ability of the institution or individual academic service unit to respond to rapid change. Solutions to problems of administration are easier to consider if the administrator is asking the right questions. In general, when evaluating both libraries and computing activities, the first question to ask is not how to, but *what for?* Since libraries or computing systems cannot be all things to all people, the administrator must ask, "What is their role within the institution?"

Midway through his research for this chapter, Donald R. Brown suffered a heart attack, which curtailed his activities. The following section is an edited version of selected notes.

R. A. Scott (Ed.). *Determining the Effectiveness of Campus Services.* New Directions for Institutional Research, no. 41. San Francisco: Jossey-Bass, March 1984.

Academic Libraries

There is no one methodology or theory directing efforts at evaluating libraries. Almost all evaluation consists of looking at expenditures for personnel and collections and the resulting size of staffs and holdings. This approach is exemplified by the annual publication of statistics by the Association of Research Libraries, whose report sets forth benchmarks for institutional library planning. The exception to this pattern is that there have been some evaluations of the use of library materials and/or library services. The best known of these studies was carried out at the University of Pittsburgh, as reported by Kent (1978). There also have been suggestions, by Morse (1968) and others, to apply systems methodology from engineering to library functions. This approach, however, has limited utility and is not likely to have any impact on libraries.

Intelligent observers could easily disagree on the priority order of specific concerns about academic libraries, but we feel that the following are three of the most important issues for which administrators should organize evaluation efforts.

1. The process by which books, serials, and other materials are selected and added to an academic library's collection needs careful scrutiny. With high inflation costs and a very unselective publication process, one basic problem is restricting acquisitions to materials that are, in fact, worth buying and storing. Unfortunately, much that is published has almost no lasting value, and much that is bought is never used.
2. Libraries need to be evaluated with regard to their ability to respond to changing information needs. New information technologies are making it possible for libraries to provide a much wider range of services and, at the same time, reduce the growth rate of costs. Automation of internal functions can reduce personnel expenditures, and the use of information technologies can make resource sharing among libraries more practical and thus more extensive. However, librarians and library managers are not likely to facilitate this class of changes.
3. The nature of the evaluation of library services needs to be evaluated. It is not useful to develop simple-minded evaluation instruments based on input measures for library functions, although such devices and strategies have been proposed. Rather, the key issue is the nature of the personnel who are responsible for library management. They must be selected in part on the basis of their ability to be evaluative. This, in turn, depends on the nature of their training and on their ability level. With the right kind of people in charge—those who are managers as well as librarians—it is likely that meaningful evaluation of both resource allocations and

functions will occur on a continuous basis and as part of normal operations.

Computing Facilities

In evaluating computing facilities, the two dimensions of major importance are what is to be evaluated and how. Since the how follows from the what, the latter is the more critical. The following are common issues facing planners.

How Much Computing Is Enough? There seems to be a widely held belief that both computing and knowing about computing are antidotes to all our national economic and educational ills. This belief even appears to extend to the conclusions that computers will change the way we think (interestingly, it is usually assumed we will think better!) and how happy we will be in our little electronic cottages. Thus, it seems that there cannot be too much of a good thing.

Is the Staff of Adequate Quality to Get the Job Done? The most important element to be evaluated in regard to computing on each campus is the quality of the staff. In order to take the next step in sophistication, research universities will have to (or want to) move to very large machines, either on campus or accessed by faculty elsewhere, and/or to complex communications networks that bring to faculty and student desks multiple processing functions. These changes require unusually sophisticated staff members. Such individuals are in very short supply nationally, and this shortage probably will be the limiting factor for campus improvements.

Research Computing Versus Instructional Computing Versus Word Processing? It is not now possible for one system of computers to serve all three masters well. At some point in the future, the single terminal may provide access to all three functions in an efficient manner.

Super Computers Versus Minis Versus Micros? It is interesting that the most exciting developments in computer systems are occurring at the two extremes—very large (super) computers and very small (personal) machines. It seems *very* likely that most major research universities will want easy access to extremely large and fast machines. This is in spite of the fact that only three institutions in the United States now have such machines on their campuses. In the future, personal computers may well become intelligent terminals with access to very large amounts of power.

Separation of Academic and Administrative Facilities? Administrators find that, in listening to urgent pleas or outraged howls from faculty, researchers, and students, opportunities abound to create complex and costly systems. But these opportunities present conflicting and highly technical problems that are difficult to assess and tricky to implement. They must be dealt with in terms of organization, management and economics, and prospects for sociological and philosophical change (Robinson, 1981). In evaluating any large-scale commitment to super computers or networking or wiring the campus, for example, what are the costs and benefits of being (too) conservative?

For universities and colleges, the two dominant attributes of the communications technology revolution are that investment in computers is being thrust upon them by external social pressures and that the investment is a large one. The widely held belief that we are becoming an information society is leading to the conclusion that all educated young people should be computer literate, which, in turn, is leading universities and colleges to try to meet that perceived need. Meeting that need is expensive. Because component costs have decreased markedly during the short lifetime of digital computers, it is often assumed that computers are cheap. That is nonsense. Cheap computers do very little computing. It is still necessary to invest $3,000 to $5,000 per student station to provide a reasonable computing environment. Evaluation of computing systems, therefore, should be a high priority item on most campuses.

Additional Issues in the Use of Computers on Campus

George Bonham (1983), executive director of the Council on Learning, has raised the following additional issues and problems to be considered:
1. The adoption of computers by schools and colleges often seems to be more cosmetic than the result of a thoughtful plan. What is your campus plan?
2. Computer literacy is a goal espoused by many educators, but is meaning seems to vary greatly. What does it mean as part of your campus mission?
3. There are many claims but little evidence about the cost-effectiveness of most computer-based learning systems. What are the costs and benefits of your proposed system?
4. If computers are to have a lasting effect on the disciplines and intellectual work in academe, we must redesign organizational and academic structures. Will this be necessary at your campus? If not, why not?

To these issues of policy and evaluation raised by Bonham, we add several others:

5. If computers are used widely as teaching aids in introductory classes, which usually have many sections, what will be the effect on the need for and support of graduate students? How will the microeconomy of graduate education be altered in the respective disciplines, and what additional support of graduate education will be needed as a consequence?
6. Is some states, more than one half of college faculty members are expected to retire, resign, or die in the next fifteen years. In what ways is your college planning to use computing as a substitute for replacing some faculty in teaching basic skills so that future faculty can become more efficient in both teaching and learning?

7. In what ways will computer hookups from the home or work place permit your campus to enroll more older, employed students who cannot attend class under current time and place restrictions?
8. Unlike books, which serve only as subjects of study in the classroom, computers may be both the source of information and the teacher of information. What incentives does your college employ to encourage faculty to develop courses that are taught and managed by computer?
9. The qualities of computers that give students and scholars access to their off-campus records also make it possible to develop programs and networks of individuals with like interests linked by computer. What plans are underway to use networks of computers to meet the needs of your campus for scarce library materials, for providing technical assistance to communities and corporations, for expanding access to educational services in still underserved areas of the state, and for mounting large-scale scientific studies?

Conclusion

The computer, both as a subject of study and as a teaching device, has great promise for transforming the ways in which we teach and learn. But, as Francis Fisher (1982, p. 6) of Haverford College, Pennsylvania, writes: "To enhance instruction and scholarship, to invest for productivity gains, to adjust for weakened restrictions of time and place, and to move ahead in the face of rapidly changing technologies and fields of competitors—we will need to do more than tinker with annual budget increments." To which we add: We need evaluation to know when some is not enough and when enough is enough.

References

Bonham, G. "Computer Mania: Academe's Inadequate Response to the Implications of the New Technology." *Chronicle of Higher Education,* March 30, 1983, p. 72.

Emery, J. C. "The Coming Challenge of Campus Computation." *EDUCOM Bulletin,* 1978, *13,* 20–23.

Fisher, F. "Teaching, Scholarship, and the Computer: Perspectives of a Generalist." *AAHE Bulletin,* November 1982, pp. 3–6.

Gillespie, R. G. "A Consensus Statement: The Panel on Computing and Higher Education." *EDUCOM Bulletin,* 1981, *16,* 20–23.

Hamblen, J. W., and Landis, C. P. (Eds.). *The Fourth Inventory of Computers in Higher Education: An Interpretive Report.* Boulder, Colorado: Westview Press, 1980.

Heydinger, R. B. "Computing and the Decision Makers: Where Does Computing Fit in Institutional Priorities? *EDUCOM Bulletin,* 1974, *9,* 2–10.

Kent, A. *A Cost-Benefit Model of Some Critical Library Operations in Terms of Use of Materials.* Final Report, NSF Grant No. SIS75-11840 and DSI75-11840A02. Pittsburgh: University of Pittsburgh, 1978.

Koenig, M. E. D. "The Information Controllability Explosion." *Library Journal,* 1982, *107,* 2052–2054.

Lancaster, F. W. *The Measurement and Evaluation of Library Services.* Arlington, Va.: Information Resources Press, 1977.

Morse, P. M. *Library Effectiveness: A Systems Approach.* Cambridge, Mass.: M.I.T. Press, 1968.

Munn, R. F. "The Bottomless Pit, or the Academic Library as Viewed from the Administration Building." *College & Research Libraries,* 1968, *29,* 51-54.

Robinson, R. J. "Computers and Information Systems for Higher Education in the 1980s: Options and Opportunities." *EDUCOM Bulletin,* 1981, *16,* 24-28.

Studer, W. J. "From Cornucopia to Famine: The Impacts and Implications of Budgetary Decline." In S. H. Lee (Ed.), *Emerging Trends in Library Organization: What Influences Change?* Ann Arbor, Mich.: Pierian Press, 1978.

Tucker, M. S. "The Turning Point: Telecommunications and Higher Education." *Journal of Communications,* 1983, *33,* 118-130.

White, H. "Library Effectiveness—The Elusive Target." *American Libraries,* 1980, *11,* 682-683.

Donald R. Brown is a research psychologist and vice-president and dean of academic services at Purdue University. He is responsible for Purdue's libraries and computing facilities.

Shirley M. Smith is assistant dean of academic services at Purdue.

Institutional change and improvement are motivated more by knowledge of problems than by knowledge of successes. Thus, negative feedback is more conducive to advancement than is positive feedback, as is evidenced by the fact that stress produced by negative performance feedback is seen as a necessary precondition for organizational learning.

Assessing Institutional Ineffectiveness: A Strategy for Improvement

Kim S. Cameron

In higher education, the concept of quality is often used interchangeably with the concept of effectiveness. With few exceptions, assessments of quality (rather than effectiveness) have dominated the educational literature, whereas the opposite is true in the literature dealing with business, government, health care, and not-for-profit organizations. Quality-based research has relied on three different approaches: reputational ratings, objective or proxy indicators, and correlates of quality rankings (see Conrad and Blackburn, 1984, for a discussion of these three approaches). The major purpose of this research has been to produce hierarchical rankings of schools based on assessments of quality and to uncover what other characteristics these high-quality schools possess. The effectiveness-based research in higher education largely has been limited to assessments of goal achievement and to assessments of the extent to which institutions possess particular effectiveness traits (see Cameron, 1978, for a discussion). This research generally has focused on identifying the most valid criteria for indicating effectiveness and the institutional processes that help predict or explain differences in effectiveness.

Both of these literatures have focused on answering the question, "How well are institutions doing?" Neither of them, however, has addressed the question, "how can institutions be made *better?*" That is, the empirical research until now has focused almost entirely on descriptions of performance, and it has not developed prescriptions for helping institutions enhance their quality or effectiveness. The literature that deals with this latter issue generally is not empirically based, and it has come mostly from the recollections of administrators or from case studies of single campuses. Unfortunately, both the empirical research and the recollections of administrators have been criticized as being unhelpful to administrators in higher education. The intent of this chapter, then, is to propose an alternative approach to institutional research that may prove useful to administrators as they try to improve the effectiveness or quality of their schools.

Institutional Effectiveness

Most of the scholarly writing on effectiveness has little practical utility (Steers, 1978) and finds its audience almost exclusively among other researchers and scholars. Administrators faced with day-to-day decisions largely ignore the debates about goal versus system resource models, which strategic constituency approach is most appropriate, the extent of rater bias, and the other theoretical and methodological issues that are typical of current effectiveness literature (Cameron and Whetten, 1983). Similarly, the effectiveness writing done by administrators on the basis of their practical experience is almost always rejected by scholars and researchers. Prescriptions for administrator action and reports of how one institution improved are seldom judged to be generalizable or valid for more than a single institution at a time. Generalizable criteria of quality or effectiveness generally are given little serious thought by these writer/practitioners. One group, therefore, is accused of being in an ivory tower and out of touch with the real world. The other group is accused of being overly simplistic and nonrigorous. Unfortunately, progress in understanding, predicting, and improving effectiveness is inhibited by the gap between these two groups.

This disparity between administrators and researchers results from the different approach each group takes toward quality or effectiveness. This difference may be illustrated by comparing institutional effectiveness to the physical health of a human being. Physical health lies on a continuum. At one end of the continuum is excellent physical health. Indicators of this condition may be a slow heart rate, high lung capacity, cardiovascular fitness, superior muscle tone, low percentage of body fat, 20/20 vision, no cavities in the teeth, and so on. At the other end of the continuum is illness, as indicated by the inability of the body to function properly and by the presence of abnormal symptoms, such as congestion, infection, bleeding, and so on. Between these two extremes is a condition of basic health, or equilibrium. The body has an absence of illness, but it may not possess the characteristics of excellent health. An individual might be overweight or out of shape, have a high relative percentage of body fat, and require glasses, but his or her physical health generally would still be considered acceptable. It is doubtful, for example, that a life insurance company would turn down such a person for a policy because of poor health. Physical health, then, is generally defined as an absence of characteristics of illness. But in order for a person to be judged in excellent health, additional characteristics have to be taken into account.

Effectiveness for colleges and universities can be considered similar to health for physical bodies. Effectiveness also lies on a continuum: At one end is high effectiveness, at the other end is ineffectivness, and in the middle lies basic effectiveness, or equilibrium. The characteristics that indicate high effectiveness are different from those that indicate ineffectiveness. That is, both the absence of characteristics of ineffectiveness and the absence of characteristics of high effectiveness indicate basic effectiveness or equilibrium. But in order to assess one end of the continuum or the other, qualitatively different characteristics must be considered.

This is also similar to Herzberg's (1959) research on individual motivation. He found that the factors individuals identified as increasing their satisfaction with their work (such as achievement, recognition, and responsibility) were different from the factors they identified as decreasing their satisfaction (such as security, pay, and supervision). Measuring satisfaction and dissatisfaction requires attention to different sets of phenomena.

On the individual health continuum, medical doctors, by and large, are concerned with criteria of illness; that is, they are concerned with eliminating disease. Physical fitness specialists (for example, professionals at health clubs) are mainly concerned with the excellent health end of the continuum — that is, with improving basic health levels. On the organizational level, administrators and practitioners are mainly concerned with the ineffectiveness end of the continuum, while researchers and theorists have focused almost exclusively on the high effectiveness end of the continuum. Administrators are faced with the problem of making their institutions operate smoothly. The elimination of institutional dysfunctions and weaknesses is a major focus of administrative behavior.

The luxury of pursuing a more excellent way is largely beyond the scope of administrators' concerns. For most administrators, then, the major concern is overcoming obstacles to basic institutional effectiveness. Researchers and theorists have been much more concerned with criteria that indicate high levels of institutional performance (Cameron, 1981). They have proposed models that focus on high-performing systems (Vaill, 1978) — that is, those systems that are more effective than the average. For example, Vaill (1981) indicates that high-performing systems are those that perform excellently against a known standard, relative to their potential, relative to their past, relative to other similar organizations, and so on. This is typical of the perspective taken by most models of effectiveness: that effective institutions perform excellently. What this orientation implies, however, is that research results and models of effectiveness in the scholarly literature may not be very helpful to administrators who are concerned with qualitatively different phenomena. Thus far, the effectiveness models "in use" frequently have focused on different criteria than have the effectiveness models "in theory" (Argyris and Schon, 1978). Because of this difference in focus, researchers have had little influence on the effectiveness of the institutions they study. As Steers (1978, p. 515) pointed out in reviewing scholarly contributions on effectiveness: "They have few answers and we already know the problems.... One could even hope that someone might have taken the trouble to suggest what all this means to the poor beleaguered manager but, alas, this is not to be found."

This largely unrecognized problem with quality and effectiveness literature—the disparity in its use by practitioners and researchers—has led to problems in trying to improve the quality of colleges and universities. Because the notion of effectiveness is different in the scholarly literature from that used by most practicing administrators, the prescriptions produced by researchers for improving effectiveness (of which there have been very few) have not been helpful to those concerned with institutional management. What is needed, therefore, is a way to combine the theoretical interests of researchers with the practical interests of practitioners to produce guidelines for administrative activity. The remainder of this chapter discusses one such alternative.

Effectiveness as an Absence of Ineffectiveness

This alternative approach to effectiveness focuses on the factors that inhibit successful institutional performance rather than on the factors that contribute to or indicate successful institutional performance (Cameron, in press). It is based on the notion that not only is it more relevant to administrators, but it is also easier and more accurate for individuals to identify criteria of ineffectiveness—that is, faults or weaknesses—than to identify criteria of effectiveness—that is, competencies or desirable outcomes.

The difficulty of identifying appropriate criteria stands as the single most important problem in effectiveness research (Brewer, 1983; Cameron, 1978; Campbell and others, 1974; Nord, 1983). Most criticism of the literature has focused on the reliability, validity, and generalizability of the criteria used in assessments. One reason for this difficulty in identifying criteria is the nature of the construct itself (Cameron, in press). Another important reason is the difficulty individuals encounter in trying to identify indicators of success (Cameron and Whetten, 1983). Van de Ven and Ferry (1980), for example, in attempting to generate criteria of effectiveness among constituencies in the Wisconsin Job Service and in some Texas childcare organizations, found that individuals had great difficulty producing effectiveness criteria "because users had not operationalized their value judgments in their own minds... [and] as might be expected, users found it impossible to formulate criteria they would use to measure intangible goals" (p. 46). They concluded that "users could not break out of their reactive role and proact [sic] by generating new effectiveness measures, even when asked to do so but not provided with a process for doing so" (p. 47). In another example, Shultz, Greenley, and Peterson (1982), in their study of hospital effectiveness, discovered that respondents found it much easier to identify weaknesses (or indicators of ineffectiveness) than strengths of their organizations (or indicators of effectiveness). Generating criteria indicating success was a major obstacle for respondents.

It also has been discovered that institutional change and improvement are motivated more by knowledge of problems than by knowledge of successes: Negative feedback is more conducive to advancement than is positive feedback. For example, Hirschman and Lindblom (1962) studied decision making in public administration, international economic development agencies, and research and engineering programs and concluded that the stress produced by negative performance feedback was the necessary precondition for organizational learning. Cangelosi and Dill (1965, p. 196), in an investigation of simulated business firm performance, concluded: "Failure, we agree, leads to change. The consequences of success, we argue, are less clear." Miles and Randolph (1980) found similar associations between organizational learning, organizational effectiveness, and negative feedback about performance: When organizations received negative rather than positive performance feedback, individuals took more responsibility for organizational outcomes, coordination of tasks became more advanced, and faster and greater quantitites of organizational learning were perceived. DeNisi, Randolph, and Blencoe (1982, p. 178), following a study of the effects of feedback on individual and group performance, concluded: "It is noteworthy that... objective performance actually improved significantly following negative individual level feedback from peers, and negative group level feedback from a superior." Stephens (1976, p. 3) concluded that individuals also are prone to agree more readily on characteristics of failure than on characteristics of success: "Analysis in terms of success, however, is much more problematic than analysis in terms of failure. Not only is it difficult to achieve consensus as to those design characteristics and functions... which lead to system success, but experience has shown that in complex systems, it is much easier to describe and achieve consensus as to what constitutes failure. When a system is functioning smoothly, it is not at all easy to specify precisely what combinations of events contribute to this state. But when breakdowns occur, they are immediately apparent, although their causes and their 'downstream' effects may be more obscure."

All this is to say that the construct of ineffectiveness, in addition to being more useful to practitioners, appears to be more easily assessed than is the construct of effectiveness. Preferences are more easily identified and more consensual. Moreover, evidence suggests that improvement is more likely in the presence of knowledge of faults than in the presence of knowledge of successes. There may be several reasons why faults in organizations are easier to identify and to reach consensus on than strengths. For example, the effects of faults are generally more obvious than are the effects of strengths in an organization. It is more obvious when things go wrong than when things are running smoothly. Individuals are more uncomfortable in the presence of organizational faults and mistakes than they are comfortable when things are right. That is, faults produce dissatisfaction on the part of individuals and efforts to reestablish equilibrium (effectiveness). An absence of faults, however, does not necessarily produce high satisfaction. It seems reasonable to suggest, then, that an approach to assessing ineffectiveness may help expand our understanding of the construct, permit potentially more accurate assessments, and prove useful to administrators by focusing on criteria that they find most relevant. Under this approach, institutional effectiveness takes on the following definition: *An institution has achieved basic effectiveness to the extent that it is free of characteristics of ineffectiveness.* As indicated earlier, qualitatively different criteria are required to assess effectiveness under this definition than to assess effectiveness under more traditional definitions that focus on the high effectiveness end of the continuum. Therefore, this definition represents a qualitatively different approach to the construct than most take, not just a flipside of the same approach. This alternative approach is based on fault tree analysis (Haasl, 1965), a procedure developed to analyze systems in the field of safety engineering.

Fault Tree Analysis

Fault tree analysis provides a well-developed procedure for systematically identifying indicators of ineffectiveness. The criteria of ineffectiveness are the faults, weaknesses, or major problems existing in an institution. The analysis focuses on these faults, therefore, instead of on indicators of institutional success. Fault tree analysis is generally thought of as a procedure for increasing the likelihood of success in any system by analyzing the most likely causes of failure (Stephens, 1972). It is a technique of reliability analysis used to diagnose potential or real problems in systems.

This procedure was developed by H. A. Watson at Bell Laboratories in 1961 (Fussell, Powers, Bennetts, 1974). Its original purpose was to evaluate the safety of the Minuteman Launch Control System in order to prevent the accidental launching of a missile. The applicability of fault tree analysis to the aerospace industry was recognized by individuals at North American Aviation (Hiltz, 1965) and at Boeing Company, so that in 1965 a symposium was held to introduce the technique to a wider audience and to acquaint others with refinements and modifications (Feutz and Waldeck, 1965; Haasl, 1965; Mearns, 1965; Michaels, 1965; Nagel, 1965). Fault tree analysis became an accepted technique of reliability analysis in safety engineering over the next ten years, but its application remained mainly in the area of nonhuman systems. Most of the literature produced on the technique discussed quantification advancements and computer program refinements. Until the mid

1970s, there were no applications of fault tree analysis to human systems, mainly because of the unreliability of predicting failures in behavior. Even now, only a handful of applications of fault tree analysis to human behavior systems have been made, and those are almost all unpublished doctoral dissertations in the field of educational administration. None of those applications, however, has considered the constructs of effectiveness, ineffectiveness, or institutional quality.

Identification of Criteria of Ineffectiveness. The first step in constructing a fault tree involves the identification of "top faults" (also called undesired events or critical failures). A top fault is a summary statement of the most crucial problem in the institution. The top fault may be a compilation of several related but more minor problems, or it may stand alone. It is essentially the answer to the question: "What is it that keeps this institution from being what it could be?" or "What is the major indicator of institutional ineffectiveness?" The top fault should be a problem that directly inhibits the institution from being more effective—that keeps it from acquiring needed resources, satisfying constituencies, or attaining goals, or that in other ways inhibits it from being judged effective. There may be several top faults in any institution, but the number of top faults considered in an analysis should be limited, since a separate fault tree must be drawn for each top fault.

A top fault should be identified in a way that maximizes the probability that it is valid and reliably identified. This is usually done through the use of a consensus-building technique, such as a nominal group or delphi, in which a variety of knowledgeable individuals identify what they consider to be the top fault(s) and then reach a consensus. Or a critical incident methodology (Flanagan, 1954) may be used, in which knowledgeable individuals are asked to agree on a critical failure event or problem in the organization's past that led to ineffectiveness. The top fault may identify a problem that *could* exist to make the organization ineffective but that doesn't exist at present. This is the general approach used in safety engineering (for instance, the radar system *could* fail). It may identify a past problem that is no longer directly present (there was a blackout power failure in New York in 1975). Or it may identify a current problem that inhibits the organization from being effective (profitability is declining). Once the top fault has been determined, it is placed at the top of the fault tree and analysis proceeds deductively.

After identifying the single most important top fault, the next step in the analysis is to identify primary faults, or factors that contribute to the occurrence or presence of the top fault. These should be factors that are directly related to the top fault in time, in space, or in other ways. This step is a critical one, because it is the primary faults that compose the branches of the fault tree. Therefore, selecting the appropriate data sources (see Cameron, 1980) is an important consideration. Fault tree analysis is not designed to analyze all possible contributing factors to the top fault—just those that are major and directly related.

One way to generate valid and reliable primary faults is to ask a group of experts—those who know well the domain being assessed—to identify the factors contributing to the top fault. Another is to analyze critical incidents as a way to discover primary faults. Other sources may be institutional records or theoretical relationships among factors shown by past research to be significant in contributing to the problem. Factors outside the institution, as well as those inside, should be considered. Because the primary faults must be directly related to the top fault, it is important that individuals who identify them be familiar with the process present in the institution. A broad representation of viewpoints is generally desirable, although it is not a prerequisite (Stephens, 1976).

Van De Ven and Ferry (1980) point out that it is frequently easier for individuals to identify the factors that cause or predict effectiveness than to identify the factors that indicate effectiveness themselves. They suggest that people generally carry around with them a model of why their organization is or isn't effective. In terms of fault tree analysis, this suggests that primary faults may be readily recoverable from the minds of experts without having to go through a rigorous system analysis. Whereas identifying the primary faults for a complete fault tree is generally time consuming, it is by no means an unreasonable task (see, for example, Barker, 1976; Driessen, 1970).

The primary faults that contribute to the top fault are listed directly below it in the tree, and they constitute the second level of the fault tree. Each of the second-level primary faults is then analyzed separately, so that the factors that contribute to their presence or occurrence in the organization are identified. That is, the analysis takes this form: The failure of A is due to $B1$, $B2$, $B3$, ... Bn; the failure of $B1$ is due to $C1$, $C2$, $C3$, ... Cn; the failure of $C1$ is due to $D1$, $D2$, $D3$, ... Dn; and so forth.

Faults on lower levels of the tree are more specific and precise than are faults on higher levels of the tree. The accuracy of fault tree analysis is generally enhanced if all primary faults on one level are identified before the next level is considered. The number of primary faults that are analyzed as contributing causes and the level of detail pursued are determined by: (1) the seven guides to conducting assessments of effectiveness discussed in Cameron and Whetten (1983)—the constituency being considered, the domain of activity, the purpose of the assessment, the level of analysis being considered, the time frame employed, the type of data available, and the referent being used; (2) the amount of information available regarding the primary faults; and (3) the amount of information needed to overcome or solve the top fault. Analysis can stop when specific change or redesign targets have been identified. Elementary fault trees may have only three or four levels of primary faults; complex trees may have as many as sixteen. (A computer program developed by Kent Stephens at Brigham Young University has been designed to handle up to sixteen levels of fault tree inputs in behaviorally oriented systems.) Each primary event need not be developed to the same level of specificity as others, however;

a fault tree many have some branches with fewer levels and other branches with many.

Relationships Among Criteria of Ineffectiveness. The key to fault tree analysis—and what makes it unique among other reliability or hierarchy analysis techniques—is the connection between faults on lower levels of the tree and faults on higher levels. These connections occur through "logic gates" derived from Boolean algebraic expressions. That is, logic gates define the relationship between lower-level faults and the faults directly above them in the tree. The Boolean logic gates most frequently used are the AND and OR expressions. The AND logic gate is used when two or more faults coexist in order to produce a more general fault. This gate is used only if all the faults are present simultaneously in order to produce a more general fault on the next higher level of the tree. For example, fault A is present only if faults B and C coexist.

The OR gate is much more common in behavioral systems, and it refers to the condition where *any* one fault on a lower level could produce the more general fault above it in the fault tree. For example, fault A is produced by either fault B or fault C. An *inclusive* OR gate indicates a situation in which B or C or both could produce A (faults are nonmutually exclusive). An *exclusive* OR gate indicates a situation in which B or C but not both could produce A (faults are mutually exclusive).

In addition to logic gates, the other types of symbols used in fault tree analysis identify the nature of the actual faults themselves. These symbols are derived from system safety engineering and are used to show the kind of primary faults that compose the fault tree analysis. There are five common types of symbols: A rectangle (☐) is the most common symbol, and it signifies a fault that results from a combination of less general faults through a logic gate. A circle (◯) signifies a fault that is at the lowest (most specific) level of analysis on the fault tree; it is a "bottom" fault. A rhombus (◇) signifies a fault that cannot be developed further because of lack of information, a remote possibility of occurrence, or some other constraint; it also is a bottom event, but not because it is sufficiently developed. A house (⌂) signifies a fault that is not normally a fault. It is a factor that is present in the organization but that does not usually indicate ineffectiveness. When combined with other faults in the tree, however, it contributes to the occurrence of a more general fault. A triangle (△) is used to indicate that a particular fault is developed further at another place in the fault tree diagram. For example, a fault may contribute to more than one general fault and so is listed more than once in the tree.

Figure 1 illustrates the use of each of these symbols in a fault tree. The tree in the figure has three branches and three levels, and it is interpreted

Figure 1. An Elementary Fault Tree Diagram

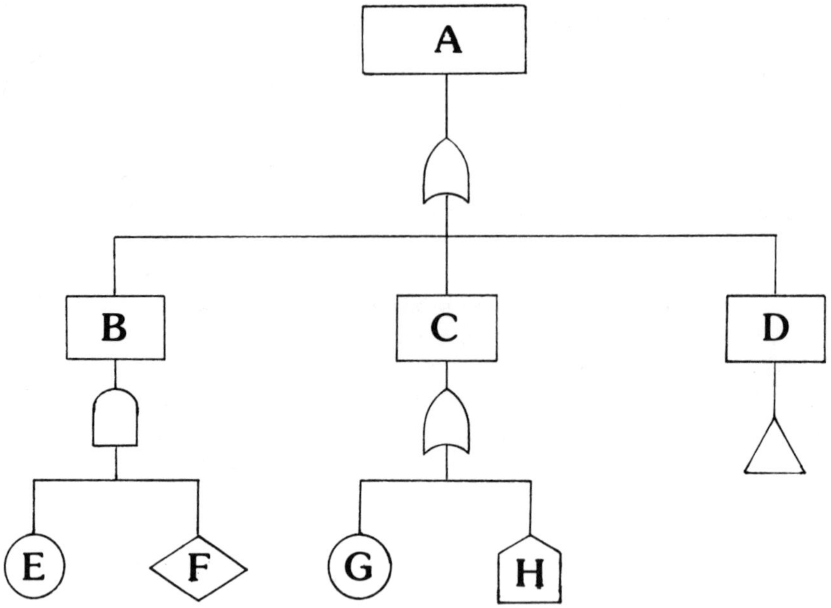

as follows: Fault A is produced by either faults B, C, D, or any combination of the three. Fault B is produced by faults E and F. Fault C is produced by faults G or H or both. Fault D is developed further at another place in the tree (not shown). Faults E and G are developed specifically as is needed in the tree. Fault F is not analyzed further because of some constraints in the analysis. Fault H is not normally an indicator of ineffectiveness, but it does contribute to the presence of fault C.

The advantage of conducting a fault tree analysis in assessing ineffectiveness is that relationships among problems within the institution are identified, and insights not normally apparent often emerge. Because a variety of alternative causes are generated, the risk of inaccurately judging a single cause-and-effect relationship is minimized. Moreover, because faults (or evidence of ineffectiveness) are being considered and not successes (or evidence of effectiveness), more specificity generally can be achieved.

Quantifying Fault Tree Analysis. The fault tree can be used to guide institutional improvement by identifying which factors in the institution should be changed in order to overcome the major cause of ineffectiveness. This is done by computing a *strategic path*. A strategic path is a route from a bottom of the tree to the top fault that identifies the faults that are most tightly linked and that most need to be changed in order to overcome ineffectiveness. This strategic path is determined by computing weights for the various faults.

The weights assigned to faults represent *probabilities*. In safety engineering, these probabilities are a product of one of two major approaches: calculation or simulation. That is, in working with hardware systems, such as a nuclear reactor, definite probabilities are associated with the occurrence of a fault or a failure. The life span of a component part, for example, can be calculated based on past experience with the part, or its life span can be determined by computer simulation (see, for example, Henley and Lynn, 1976). With both of these procedures, however, it is assumed that an objective probability actually exists for each fault, and the analyst's job is to estimate that probability as accurately as possible. In behavioral systems (such as organizations), however, objective probabilities are not associated with specific faults, and they cannot be determined either by calculating past event probabilities or by simulation. Therefore, different methods are required in order to assign weights.

There are a variety of alternatives for assigning weights to the faults in a fault tree. For example, Srinivasan and Shocker (1973) reviewed ten such procedures that had earlier been introduced by Sluckin (1956) and by Blum and Naylor (1968). The best procedure for determining a strategic path in behavior systems, however, was introduced by Stephens (1972). It involves the use of consensual expert ratings to estimate the relative contribution or *importance* of the fault, and the *frequency* of fault occurrence (its urgency). Obtaining consensual ratings helps maximize the reliability and validity of the assigned weights.

The rating of the importance of faults is done via a consensus-building approach such as nominal-group or delphi techniques according to their relative contributions to a more general fault. A percentage contribution is assigned to the faults on each level of the tree. That is, the weightings of all the contributing faults on one level of one branch of the tree should sum to 1.00. If fault A is caused by faults B and C, for example, the rating of the importance of faults B and C must sum to 1.0 (fault B = .6 and fault C = .4). Asking individuals to assign quantified values to their ratings is consistent with the advice of Kotler (1970, p. 80): "Executives and experts who are asked to put their judgments in the form of numbers tend to give harder thought to the problem, especially if the numbers are a matter of record.... Quantification helps pinpoint the extent and importance of differences among executives with respect to the decision problem. Numbers permit the analyst to perform a sensitivity analysis to determine how much a decision depends on particular differences in judgment."

Judgments regarding the frequency of occurrence of the fault are made only for bottom faults. This is because the frequency of occurrence for more general faults (or the urgency with which they must be addressed) is a function of the frequency of the faults on lower levels. It may be the case that not all frequently occurring lower faults contribute to the occurrence of a higher fault. But, if the fault tree is constructed properly and the faults on the lower levels of the tree are identified as having a causal relationship to the faults immediately above them, the logic of this computational formula holds.

Estimates of frequency are produced by having experts assign probabilities to faults based on a scale of how often they occur (for example, frequently = .8, seldom = .5, never = .2). Each fault is rated independently—unlike the ratings of relative contribution, which are rated in relation to one another—so that weights need not sum to 1.0 for each set of contributing faults. The scale used for the ratings depends largely on researcher preference, as long as it makes sense relative to the faults being analyzed. The weighting assigned to the bottom faults is a product of the expert estimates of importance and frequency (importance x freqency). It signifies the relative contribution of that particular fault to the occurrence of the fault on the next highest level of the tree.

Having weights assigned to each primary fault in the tree now permits the computation of the strategic path. In safety engineering, the strategic path represents the weakest links in the system, or the areas in which failure is most probable. In colleges and universities, it identifies the interactions among the most important problems in the institution that inhibit institutional effectiveness. Computing the strategic path helps identify guidelines for implementing organizational redesign that eliminates or overcomes faults. Strategic paths are identified by using Boolean algebraic formulas (the algebra of events) to compute weights for each connecting logic gate in the tree, beginning at the lowest levels in the tree. The weights of the individual faults are used as the basis for the computations. (For a detailed explanation of these formulas and how to use them, see Cameron, in press.)

The advantage of quantifying the strategic paths rather than simply estimating them is that more precise and more accurate analyses result (Kotler, 1970; Wood, Stephens, and Barker, 1979) and a clear strategy for improvement is specified. In complex fault trees, it is not always clear where institutional improvement should begin because of the sheer number of contributing faults in the tree. The formulas derived from Boolean algebra, therefore, are designed to make precise the couplings among the faults in the tree and to identify which faults should be overcome first. Therefore, if the fault tree has been properly constructed and the bottom faults are sufficiently precise so as to be alterable, the strategic path maps a way to improve institutional effectiveness by eliminating ineffectiveness. The power of fault tree analysis may be enhanced if it is used as an iterative process. That is, when procedures have been employed to eliminate faults along the strategic path, the relative weightings of other faults in the tree may change. A new analysis may uncover a new strategic path that was not identified in the earlier fault tree. Continuous self-analysis in an institution, then, could enhance the self-design and self-renewal process.

Advantages and Disadvantages

It has been argued that, because practitioners and researchers use different conceptualizations of effectiveness or quality, most scholarly writing is of little use in guiding institutional improvement. An alternative view of effectiveness or quality, along with a methodology for assessing it, was presented, however, in order to combine systematic analysis with administrators' needs to increase the effectiveness of their institutions. This alternative approach has several advantages and disadvantages.

Advantages. One advantage of this approach is that is is easier to agree on faults, problems, and weaknesses of institutions than on their strengths or successes. Particularly in such complex organizations as universities, in which goals are difficult to identify and preferences regarding what the organization should be pursuing vary among constituencies, agreement about what the organization should avoid is much more easily specified. A second advantage is that a focus on criteria of ineffectiveness is congruent with administrator concerns. It helps fill the void that has existed in much of the literature on quality and effectiveness regarding administrator problems. Since overcoming institutional problems and faults constitutes a large part of administrator behavior, this approach helps tie together researcher analysis with administrator requirements.

A third advantage is that broad participation by institutional members in both the diagnosis and assessment and the identification of strategies for improved effectiveness helps avoid dysfunctional consequences of rigorous research (see Argyris, 1968). In traditional assessments that rely on questionnaire responses or structured interviews, misinformation or inadequate information, rejecting or ignoring the findings, second guessing the study design, and other forms of resistance are common occurrences (Cameron, 1978). In this approach, both analysts and institutional participants learn collaboratively about the criteria under investigation.

A fourth advantage is that an understanding of the institution and the interrelationships among its subparts is enhanced by this approach. The interrelationships among factors that contribute to weakness and ineffectiveness in the institution are made clearer by engaging in fault tree analysis. Effective institutional change is therefore enhanced. A fifth advantage of this approach is that it combines description with prescription. The fault tree approach not only serves descriptive purposes—describing the current state of institutional performance—but it also serves a prescriptive or normative purpose as well—generating strategies for improvement. Therefore, improving effectiveness and assessing effectiveness are products of the same analysis.

A sixth advantage is that this approach can be used to assess institutional potentialities as well as current levels of functioning. Brewer (1983), Mohr (1983), and Nord (1983) imply that not only should evaluations of effectiveness focus on what organizations do produce, but consideration also should be given to what they could produce. A fault tree analysis can be constructed in the future tense and analyzed in terms of the major indicators of ineffectiveness that could occur in the institution. Change strategies are then recommended to prevent ineffectiveness from occurring.

Disadvantages. Of course, focusing on ineffectiveness through fault tree analysis also may have drawbacks. It is not an approach that resolves all of the problems of linking institutional improvement to assessments of institutional effectiveness. At least five potential disadvantages exist. First, information may not exist regarding all the institution's major faults. Contributing faults on lower levels of a fault tree may be difficult to uncover, and underlying causes of problems may not be apparent or may be inaccurately assumed. Identifying some faults may even be the result of political processes, so that different fault trees may be produced depending on which group is asked. For example, constituencies may identify only those faults that place blame on other groups or on uncontrollable factors so as to relieve themselves of responsibility for weaknesses in the institution or of a need for change.

Second, constructing accurate fault trees may take many hours and involve many people. It is certainly not as easy as sending out a questionnaire to administrators or faculty in a sample of institutions and then tabulating the results. Moreover, fault tree analysis, as currently developed, is limited to one unit of analysis, and comparisons among institutions require separate fault trees for each institution. Fault tree analysis focuses more on improving a single unit than on making comparisons among multiple units.

Third, there is no guarantee that solving a problem on a lower level of the fault tree will automatically solve the problem to which it contributes on an upper level of the tree. Whereas fault tree analysis can identify the faults that are most tightly coupled in the tree and that contribute most to ineffectiveness, it does not guarantee that a domino effect will result from solving one bottom fault. Moreover, no empirical work has been published to date demonstrating that the faults identified along the strategic path are, in fact, the most powerful in overcoming the top fault. Anecdotal evidence has appeared in several articles, but it is not certain that intuitive judgments or a random selection of solutions would not be just as efficacious as rigorous fault tree analysis for overcoming or eliminating the top fault. This is an area in which further research is needed.

Fourth, this approach pays attention not to institutional strengths but to institutional weaknesses. Some policy analysts suggest that organizations are better off focusing resources and organizational energies on what is done well. That focus advocates capitalizing on what is successful already. Resources should not be plowed into problem areas, according to that view. This approach takes the opposite stance by defining effectiveness as the absence of ineffectiveness. It advocates concentrating on organizational weaknesses in order to overcome them, which implies a reallocation of resources in problematic areas. The relative efficacy of overcoming weaknesses versus magnifying strengths is another unknown but fruitful area for future research.

Fifth, some kinds of organizations function well because they are *not* understood very well. Colleges and universities are among such organizations. These organizations have loose coupling, nonexistent or fuzzy goals, fluid structures, and so on. The advantage of this kind of design is that discretion is maximized and multiple demands can be addressed at once. Two problems may occur in this kind of organization, however, because of fault tree analysis. First, relationships among faults that are identified by fault tree analysis may be too loosely coupled and dynamic to allow for a reliable analysis. Second, fault tree analysis may lead to institutional change that produces tighter couplings than were intended. No organization is a completely rational system, but the fault tree procedure treats organizations as if at least some couplings are relatively tight and procedures are rational. The extent to which this treatment is helpful or harmful is a subject of needed empirical investigation.

Despite these potential disadvantages, the analysis of ineffectiveness through a fault tree presents a potentially useful alternative for overcoming the current gaps between scholarly and administrative approaches to successful institutional performance. Until now, there has been a wide gap between the needs of researchers to assess quality and effectiveness and the needs of administrators to improve quality and effectiveness. Fault tree analysis provides one alternative for making those needs more compatible.

References

Argyris, C. "Some Unintended Consequences of Rigorous Research." *Psychological Bulletin,* 1968, *70,* 185-197.

Argyris, C., and Schon, D. *Organizational Learning: A Theory of Action Perspective.* Reading Mass.: Addison-Wesley, 1978.

Barker, B.O. "Fault Tree Analysis: Its Implicatons for Use in Education." Unpublished master's thesis, Utah State University, 1976.

Blum, M. L., and Naylor, J. C. *Industrial Psychology: Its Theoretical and Social Foundations.* New York: Harper & Row, 1968.

Brewer, G. D. "Assessing Outcomes and Effects." In K. S. Cameron and D. A. Whetten (Eds.), *Organizational Effectiveness: A Comparison of Multiple Models.* New York: Academic Press, 1983.

Cameron, K. S. "Measuring Organizational Effectiveness in Institutions of Higher Education." *Administrative Science Quarterly,* 1978, *23,* 604-632.

Cameron, K. S. "Critical Questions in Assessing Organizational Effectiveness." *Organizational Dynamics,* 1980, *9,* 66-80.

Cameron, K. S. "Domains of Organizational Effectiveness in Colleges and Universities." *Academy of Management Journal,* 1981, *24,* 25-47.

Cameron, K. S. "The Effectiveness of Ineffectiveness." In B. M. Staw and L. L. Cummings (Eds.), *Research in Organizational Behavior.* Greenwich, Conn.: JAI Press, in press.

Cameron, K. S., and Whetten, D. A. *Organizational Effectiveness: A Comparison of Multiple Models.* New York: Academic Press, 1983.

Campbell, J. P., Brownas, E. A., Peterson, N. G., and Dunnette, M. D. *The Measurement of Organizational Effectiveness: A Review of Relevant Research and Opinion.* Final report, Navy Personnel Research and Development Center. Minneapolis: Personnel Decisions, 1974.

Cangelosi, V. E., and Dill, W. R. "Organizational Learning: Observations Toward a Theory." *Administrative Science Quarterly,* 1965, *10,* 175-203.

Conrad, C., and Blackburn, R. "Program Quality in Higher Education: A Review and Critique of Literature and Research." In J. Smith (Ed.), *Annual Handbook of Higher Education.* Vol. 1. Blacksburg: Virginia Polytechnic Institute and State University, 1984, forthcoming.

DeNisi, A. S., Randolph, W. A., and Blencoe, A. G. "Level and Score of Feedback as Determinants of Feedback Effectiveness." *Academy of Management Proceedings,* 1982, 175-179.

Driessen, G. J. "Cause Tree Analysis: Measuring How Accidents Happen and the Probabilities of Their Causes." Paper presented at the 78th Annual Meeting of the American Psychological Association, Miami Beach, Fla., September 1970.

Feutz, R. J., and Waldeck, T. A. "The Application of Fault Tree Analysis to Dynamic Systems." Paper presented at Systems Safety Symposium, Seattle, June 15, 1965.

Flanagan, J. C. "The Critical Incident Technique." *Psychological Bulletin,* 1954, *51,* 327-358.

Fussell, J. B., Powers, G. J., and Bennetts, R. "Fault Tree: A State of the Art Discussion." *Institute for Electrical and Electronics Engineering Transactions on Reliability,* April 1974, R-23, 51-55.

Haasl, D. F. "Advanced Concepts in Fault Tree Analysis." Paper presented at Systems Safety Symposium, Seattle, June 15, 1965.

Henley, E. J., and Lynn, J. W. *Generic Techniques in Systems Reliability Assessment.* Leyden, Netherlands: Noordhoff, 1976.

Herzberg, F., Mausner, B., and Synderman, B. *The Motivation to Work.* New York: Wiley, 1959.

Hiltz, P. A. *The Fundamentals of Fault Tree Analysis.* Downey, Calif.: North American Aviation, 1965.

Hirschman, A. O., and Lindblom, C. E. "Economic Development, Research and Development, Policy Making: Some Converging Views." *Behavioral Science,* 1962, *8,* 211-222.

Kotler, P. "A Guide to Gathering Expert Estimates." *Business Horizons,* 1970, *13,* 79-87.

Mearns, A. B. "Fault Tree Analysis: The Study of Unlikely Events in Complex Systems." Paper presented at Systems Safety Symposium, Seattle, June 15, 1965.

Michaels, J. M. "Computer Evaluation of the Safety Fault Tree Model." Paper presented at Systems Safety Symposium, Seattle, June 15, 1965.

Miles, R. H., and Randolph, A. "Influence of Organizational Learning Styles on Early Development." In J. R. Kimberly, R. H. Miles, and Associates (Eds.), *The Organizational Life Cycle: Issues in the Creation, Transformation, and Decline of Organizations.* San Francisco: Jossey-Bass, 1980.

Mohr, L. R. "The Implications of Effectiveness Theory for Managerial Practice in the Public Sector." In K. S. Cameron and D. A. Whetten (Eds.), *Organizational Effectiveness: A Comparison of Multiple Models.* New York: Academic Press, 1983.

Nagel, P. M. "A Monte Carlo Method to Compute Fault Tree Probabilities." Paper presented at Systems Safety Symposium, Seattle, June 15, 1965.

Nord, W. R. "A Political-Economic Perspective on Organizational Effectiveness." In K. S. Cameron and D. A. Whetten (Eds.), *Organizational Effectiveness: A Comparison of Multiple Models.* New York: Academic Press, 1983.

Powers, G. J. "Fault Tree Synthesis for Chemical Process. *American Institute of Chemical Engineering,* 1974, *20,* 376-387.

Shultz, R., Greenley, J., and Peterson, R. *Why Do Some Health Services Provide Quality Care and/or Private Care at Lower Costs Than Others?* Madison: Department of Preventive Medicine, University of Wisconsin-Madison, 1982.

Sluckin, W. "Combining Criteria of Occupational Stress." *Occupational Psychology,* (Part 1). 1956, *30,* 20-26. Part 2, 1956, *30,* 57-67.

Srinivasan, V., and Shocker, A. D. "Linear Programming Techniques for Multidimensional Analysis of Preferences." *Psychometrika,* 1973, *38,* 337-369.

Steers, R. M. Review of S. L. Spray (Ed.), *Organizational Effectiveness: Theory, Research, and Application* (Kent, Ohio: Kent State University Press, 1976) and P. S. Goodman,

J. M. Pennings, and Associates (Eds.), *New Perspectives on Organizational Effectiveness* (San Francisco: Jossey-Bass, 1977). *Administrative Science Quarterly,* 1978, *23,* 512-515.

Stephens, K. G. "A Fault Tree Approach to Analysis of Systems as Demonstrated in Vocational Education." Unpublished doctoral dissertation, University of Washington, 1972.

Stephens, K. G. "A Fault Tree Approach to Needs Assessment—An Overview." Paper presented at Needs Assessment Conference, Oakland, California, April 8, 1976.

Vaill, P. B. "Toward a Behavioral Description of High Performing Systems." In M. McCall and M. Lombardo (Eds.), *Leadership: Where Else Can We Go?* Durham, N.C.: Duke University Press, 1978.

Vaill, P. B. "The Purposing of High Performing Systems." Paper presented at conference on Administrative Leadership: New Perspectives on Theory and Practice, University of Illinois, Urbana, July 17-18, 1981.

Van De Ven, A. H., and Ferry, D. *Measuring and Assessing Organizations.* New York: Wiley, 1980.

Wood, R. K., Stephens, K. G., and Barker, B. O. "Fault Tree Analysis: An Emerging Methodology for Instructional Science." *Instructional Science,* 1979, *8,* 1-22.

Kim S. Cameron is director of organizational studies at the National Center for Higher Education Management Systems. The research reported in this chapter was conducted under a contract (#400-80-0109) with the National Institute for Education.

A final synthesis and suggestions about additional resources.

Concluding Notes and Further Readings

Robert A. Scott

The topic of effectiveness has reached new levels of popularity. It is the subject of best-selling books as well as pamphlets and articles designed for particular audiences. It also appears in national reports on subjects as diverse as manufacturing and schooling. While many of the books and articles on effectiveness or quality seem to be aimed at those involved in business of one sort or another, there are also special efforts directed toward leaders in the fields of health, social services, government, and education.

One of the more interesting of the business-oriented books is the volume on excellence and innovation by Peters and Waterman (1982). In it, the authors discuss the characteristics of effectiveness in sixty-two American corporations, which are identified as having been highly successful over a twenty-year period in terms of both growth and such absolute measures of economic health as profits, market share, and return on investment. In describing their definition of effectiveness, the authors take pains to point out that they purposefully did not try to be too precise for fear of losing the essence of what they were after. In this regard, they quote E. B. White's account of humor, which, according to White, "can be dissected, as a frog, but the thing dies in the process and the innards are discouraging to any but the pure scientific mind" (Peters and Waterman, 1982, p. 19). Instead, the authors asked an informed group of observers of the business scene—executives, consultants, members of the business press, and business academics—to list the names of companies that they thought were innovative in terms of both products and responses to shifts in the marketplace and thus were worthy of being considered excellent. Among the lessons learned by Peters and Waterman is that organizational effectiveness is directly related to management action. This is the same lesson learned from Cameron's work on educational institutions—a lesson that is underscored in the preceding chapters.

This theme of organizational effectiveness as a consequence of managerial action is one of two that are central to this volume. The other theme is that assessments of services are assessments of staff. Whether one's concern is assessing a self-study process, student services, public relations, a cooperative venture with industry, or library and computing facilities, the assessment of staff eventually becomes a central concern.

According to Fisher (1977a, p. 4), "the [staff] evaluation process is a review of performance *vis-a-vis* goal expectations and individual potential through the use of appropriate assessment techniques that involve those persons with whom the individual interacts so as to determine areas of needed and desired professional development." However, as closely entwined as staff performance and program or service effectiveness are, one must strive to keep them separate. Lehmann (1981, p. 769) comments on this need for separation in order to have effective program evaluation: "The staff running a particular program will cooperate more fully and be more interested in the results if it is clear from the outset that the program itself is the target of evaluation.... If staff evaluation is mixed with program evaluation, the staff's natural inclination to emphasize the positive may seriously distort the evaluation. Personnel evaluation of program staff should either follow the regular personnel practices of the campus or be conducted separately from any program evaluation effort, according to procedures established at the start of the new program (or the start of the new service year)."

Nevertheless, there are linkages to be made between professional development or renewal, as opposed to personnel evaluation, and the assessment of campus services. Those individuals who assume leadership in the assessment of a service are undertaking a significant responsibility, which is itself a form of professional development that can lead to staff renewal. This is a rarely recognized form of staff development (Lehmann, 1981, p. 769).

Some especially useful sources on this form of staff evaluation are noted in the following reference section.

References

Anderson, S. B., Ball, S., Murphy, R. T., and Associates. *Encyclopedia of Educational Evaluation: Concepts and Techniques for Evaluating Education and Training Programs.* San Francisco: Jossey-Bass, 1975.

Delworth, U., Hanson, G. R., and Associates. *Student Services: A Handbook for the Profession.* San Francisco: Jossey-Bass, 1980.

Dressel, P. L. *Administrative Leadership: Effective and Responsive Decision Making in Higher Education.* San Francisco: Jossey-Bass, 1981.

Fincher, C. "Linking Faculty Evaluation and Faculty Rewards in the University." *Issues in Higher Education,* Number 16, 1980, 1-7.

Fisher, C. (Ed.). *Developing and Evaluating Administrative Leadership.* New Directions for Higher Education, no. 22. San Francisco: Jossey-Bass, 1978.

Fisher, C. "The Evaluation and Development of College and University Administrators." *ERIC/Higher Education Research Currents.* March 1977a; June 1977b.

Galvin, T. J., and Lynch, B. P. (Eds.). *Priorities for Academic Libraries.* New Directions for Higher Education, no. 39. San Francisco: Jossey-Bass, 1982.

Goodman, P. S., Pennings, J. M., and Associates. *New Perspectives on Organizational Effectiveness.* San Francisco: Jossey-Bass, 1977.

Guba, E. G., and Lincoln, Y. S. *Effective Evaluation: Improving the Usefulness of Evaluation Results Through Responsive and Naturalistic Approaches.* San Francisco: Jossey-Bass, 1981.

Jedamus, P., Peterson, M. W., and Associates. *Improving Academic Management: A Handbook of Planning and Institutional Research.* San Francisco: Jossey-Bass, 1980.

Kirschling, W. R. (Ed.). *Evaluating Faculty Performance and Vitality.* New Directions for Institutional Research, no. 20. San Francisco: Jossey-Bass, 1978.

Lehmann, T. "Evaluating Adult Learning and Program Costs." In A. Chickering and Associates, *The Modern American College: Responding to the New Realities of Diverse Students and a Changing Society.* San Francisco: Jossey-Bass, 1981.

McCorkle, C. O., Jr., and Archibald, S. O. *Management and Leadership in Higher Education: Applying Modern Techniques of Planning, Resource Management, and Evaluation.* San Francisco: Jossey-Bass, 1982.

Nordvall, R. C. *Evaluation and Development of Administrators.* AAHE-ERIC/Higher Education Research Report No. 6. Washington, D.C.: ERIC Clearinghouse on Higher Education, 1979.

Peters, T. J., and Waterman, R. H. *In Search of Excellence: Lessons from America's Best-Run Companies.* New York: Harper & Row, 1982.

Poulton, N. L. (Ed.). *Evaluation of Management and Planning Systems.* New Directions for Institutional Research, no. 31. San Francisco: Jossey-Bass, 1981.

Reid, J. Y. "Politics and Quality in Administrator Evaluation." *Research in Higher Education,* 1982, *16* (1), 27-40.

Strider, R. E. "Checking out Presidential Assessment." *AGB Reports,* 1982, *24* (1), 54-56.

Robert A. Scott is director of academic affairs for the Indiana Commission for Higher Education.

Index

A

Accreditation: constituencies for, 11; and institutional self-study, 12-21; national importance of, 11-12; regional, and quality, 10-12
Administration, bibliography on evaluation of, 7
Admissions, open, and student services, 27
Allen, R. P., 41, 49
American College Personnel Association, 25
American Council on Education, 4-5, 6, 24
Anderson, S. B., 7, 86
Anna Maria College, public relations at, 45
Appalachian State University, public relations at, 46
Archibald, S. O., 87
Argyris, C., 70, 79, 81
Association of Research Libraries, 62
Astin, A. W., 31, 33, 35

B

Ball, S., 7, 86
BanSlyke, J. K., 38-39, 49
Barker, B. O., 74, 78, 81, 83
Barnett, L., 5
Baugher, D., 7
Bell Laboratories, 72
Bennetts, R., 72, 82
Bethel College, public relations at, 45
Blackburn, R., 67, 81
Blencoe, A. G., 71, 82
Blum, M. L., 77, 81
Boeing Company, 72
Bonham, G., 64, 65
Borden Company, 41
Brewer, G. D., 70, 79, 81
Briarcliff College, public relations at, 45
Brown, D. R., 6, 61-66
Brownas, E. A., 81
Buena Vista College, public relations at, 45
Business. *See* Industry-education alliance

C

California, University of, student services fees at, 33
California at Berkeley, University of: and industry, 58; minority student services at, 28
Cameron, K. S., 2-4, 5, 6, 67-83, 86
Campbell, J. B., 70, 81
Campus services, self-study for enhancing, 9-22
Cangelosi, V. I., 71, 81
Carnegie Council on Policy Studies in Higher Education, 23, 35
Carnegie-Mellon University: and industry, 58; public relations at, 41, 46
Caruthers, J. K., 17-18, 21
Centra, J. A., 6
Central College, public relations at, 45
Chambers, R. H., 5, 9-22
Chapman College, public relations at, 44
Chickering, A. W., 18, 21
Ciervo, A., 40, 42, 49, 50
Clark, B. R., 13, 21
College and University Environmental Scales, 31
College Board, Student Search Service, 47
College Characteristics Index, 31
College Student Experiences, 32
Columbia University, faculty at, 19
Committee on Student Personnel Services, 24, 35
Community College Goals Inventory, 31
Commuter students, services for, 27
Computing facilities, assessing, 63-66
Conrad, C., 67, 81
Control Data, 58
Corbitt, T., 50
Council for Advancement and Support of Education, 38
Council of Independent Colleges (CIC), 39, 45, 50
Council on Postsecondary Accreditation, 10
Craemer, D. G., 25, 35
Craven, E., 7

89

D

Darwin, C., 9
Delworth, U., 86
De Nisi, A. S., 71, 82
Dickinson College, public relations at, 43
Dill, W. R., 71, 81
Dominican College, public relations at, 45
Dressel, P. L., 2, 6, 13, 19, 20, 21, 34, 35, 87
Driessen, G. J., 74, 82
Dunnette, M. D., 81
du Pont, P., IV, 53

E

Education, public concerns about, 51-52. *See also* Industry-education alliance
Educational Testing Service, 31
Effectiveness: as absence of ineffectiveness, 70-72; assessing, 13; and concept of quality, 67; dimensions of, 3; evaluation of, 1; guides for assessing, 74; and innovation, 85-86; institutional, 68-70; measures of, 2-4; and staff, 86
Eisenhower, D. D., 19
Emery, J. C., 65
Emhart Corporation, 58
Enarson, H. L., 10, 22
Evaluation: as education, 13-15; features of, 1; and quality, 32-35

F

Faculty: bibliography on evaluation of, 6; self-study attention to, 19
Fairman, J., 41, 50
Fault tree analysis: advantages of, 79; and criteria of ineffectiveness, 73-75; disadvantages of, 79-81; and logic gates, 75; process of, 72-78; quantifying, 76-78; relationships in, 75-76; strategic path in, 76-77
Feasley, C. E., 7
Feedback, negative and positive, 71
Ferry, D., 70-71, 74, 83
Feutz, R. J., 72, 82
Fincher, C., 13, 22, 87
Fisher, C., 7, 86, 87

Fisher, F., 65
Flanagan, J. C., 73, 82
Franklin Partnership, 59
Friends University, public relations at, 45
Fussell, J. B., 72, 82

G

Galvin, T. J., 87
Georgetown University, public relations at, 49
Georgia Institute of Technology, Technology Development Center at, 58
Gettysburg College, public relations at, 41
Gillespie, R. G., 65
Girrell, K. W., 27, 35
Goldberg, E. D., 7, 13, 16, 22
Goodman, P. S., 87
Graduate Record Examination, 32
Greenley, J., 71, 82
Guba, E. G., 87

H

Haasl, D. F., 72, 82
Halstead, C. P., 5, 37-50
Hamblen, J. W., 65
Hanson, G. R., 32, 35, 86
Harpel, R. L., 30, 35
Havighurst, R. J., 21
Henley, E. J., 77, 82
Herzberg, F., 69, 82
Heydinger, R. B., 65
Hiltz, P. A., 72, 82
Hirschman, A. O., 71, 82
Hoyt, D. P., 7
Hutchins, R., 2, 6

I

IBM, 58
Industry-education alliance: assessing, 51-60; assumptions in, 56; background on, 52-53; consortia for, 58-59; evaluation of, 57; examples of, 57-59; next steps for, 59; and personnel exchanges, 58; planning for, 54-57; research and development in, 58; steps in, 56-57; trends leading to, 53-54

Ineffectiveness: absence of, as effectiveness, 70-72; assessing, 67-83; criteria of, 73-75; fault tree analysis for, 72-81; relationships among criteria of, 75-76
Inman, B., 54
Innovation: and effectiveness, 85-86; openness to, 19-20
Institutional advancement. *See* Public relations
Institutional Functioning Inventory, 31
Institutional Goals Inventory, 31

J

Jacobson, H. K., 38, 48, 50
Jacoby, B., 27, 35
Jedamus, P., 87

K

Kansas Wesleyan College, and industry, 58
Kauffman, J. F., 5, 23-36
Kells, H. R., 15, 17, 21, 22, 33, 35
Kent, A., 62, 65
Kirschling, W. C., 6, 87
Koenig, M. E. D., 65
Kotler, P., 38, 50, 78, 82
Kuh, G. D., 18, 22

L

Lancaster, F. W., 66
Landis, C. P., 65
Lee, Y. S., 36
Lehmann, T., 1, 6, 57, 60, 86, 87
Lenning, O. T., 32, 36
Leonard, E. A., 24, 36
Leone, A. O., 7, 13, 16, 22
Libraries, assessing, 62-63
Lincoln, Y. S., 87
Lindblom, C. E., 71, 82
Lynch, B. P., 87
Lynn, J. W., 77, 82

M

McCorkle, C. O., Jr., 87
March, J., 2, 6
Marcus, L. R., 7, 13, 16, 22
Marville, A., 28, 36
Maryland, University of, commuter student services at, 27
Massachusetts Institute of Technology, and industry, 54
Mausner, B., 82
Mearns, A. B., 72, 82
Meek, E., 43, 44, 50
Micek, S. S., 36
Michaels, J. M., 72, 82
Middle States Association of Colleges and Schools, 14, 16, 18, 20, 22
Miles, R. H., 71, 82
Millard, R. M., 9-10, 11, 17, 22
Minority students, services for, 27-28
Minuteman Launch Control System, 72
Mission: clarity of, 17-18; and student satisfaction, 18; student services related to, 26-28
Mississippi, University of, public relations at, 43, 44
Mohr, L. R., 79, 82
Moore, R. K., 41, 46, 50
Morse, P. M., 62, 66
Munn, R. F., 66
Murphy, R. T., 86

N

Nagel, P. M., 72, 82
National Association of Public Affairs and Administration, 16
National Association of Student Personnel Administrators (NASPA), 28
National Center for Higher Education Management Systems (NCHEMS), 32
Naylor, J. C., 77, 81
Nies, T. N., 54
Nord, W. R., 70, 79, 82
Nordvall, R. C., 7, 87
North American Aviation, 72

O

Oberlin College, nature of, 29
O'Brien, P., 51, 60
Olsen, J., 2, 6
Olson, G. S., 28, 36
Orwell, G., 19

P

Pace, C. R., 32, 36
Parker, L., 44, 50

Pennings, J. M., 87
Pennsylvania, industry-education consortium in, 58-59
Pennsylvania State University, public relations at, 40, 41-42
Peters, T. J., 85-86, 87
Peterson, M. W., 87
Peterson, N. G., 81
Peterson, R., 71, 82
Pirsig, R. M., 9, 22
Pittsburgh, University of, library evaluation at, 62
Plough, T. R., 30, 36
Poulton, N. L., 87
Powell, S., 5-6, 51-60
Powers, G. J., 72, 82
Princeton University, Forrestal Center at, 58
Programs, bibliography on evaluation of, 7
Public relations: assessing, 37-50; audiences for, 43-44; and communication channels, 46-47; criteria for evaluating, 39-50; evaluating, 47-49; function of, 38-39; goals for, 40-41; messages and themes in, 44-45; objectives for, 41-42; planning of, 39-40; priorities for, 42; response to, 49; strategy for, 45-46
Purdue University, and industry, 58

Q

Quality: and accreditation, 10-12; candor and integrity linked to, 12-13; and concept of effectiveness, 67; defining, 9-10, 29-31; and evaluation, 32-35

R

Randolph, A., 71, 82
Randolph, W. A., 71, 82
Reid, J. R., 87
Rentz, C. C., 7
Rentz, R. R., 7
Research, bibliography on evaluation of, 7
Robinson, R. J., 63, 66
Ross, J., 43, 50

S

Schon, D., 70, 81
Scott, R. A., 1-7, 10, 16, 22, 61-66, 85-87
Self-study, institutional: analysis of, 12-21; assessing, 20-21; for assessing effectiveness, 13; candor, integrity, and quality linked in, 12-13; comprehensive and topical types of, 18-19; continuous, 15; and evaluation as education, 13-15; faculty attended to by, 19; and innovation, 19-20; institutional components in, 15-17; leadership for, 17; and mission clarity, 17-18; purpose of, 12; quality enhancement through, 9-22; questions for, 14; steering committee for, 20; and student services, 32, 33
Semi-Conductor Research Corporation, 58
Semrow, J. J., 14, 22
Service, A. L., 36
Shocker, A. D., 77, 82
Shultz, R., 71, 82
Skelly, G., 43, 44, 50
Sluckin, W., 77, 82
Smith, N., 27-28, 36
Smith, S. M., 6, 61-66
Sohio, 58
Spencer, H., 9
Srinivasan, V., 77, 82
Stanford University, and industry, 54, 58
Steers, R. M., 68, 70, 82-83
Stephens, K. G., 71, 72, 74, 77, 78, 83
Strider, R. E., 87
Student services: and academic environment, 28-29; assessing quality of, 23-36; basic, 25-26; defining quality in, 29-31; evaluation of, and quality, 32-35; evolution of, 24-25; and information about students, 31-32; mission related to, 26-28; and self-studies, 32, 33
Students: changing types of, 23; disabled, services for, 28; foreign, services for, 28; information on, 31-32; returning adult, services for, 27; satisfaction of, and mission, 18
Studer, W. J., 66
Synderman, B., 82

T

Texas at Austin, University of, and industry, 54
Thies, A. H., 42, 50
Truitt, R. H., 41, 50
TRW, 58
Tucker, M. S., 66

U

University Residence Environment Scales, 31-32

V

Vaill, P. B., 69, 83
Van De Ven, A. H., 70-71, 74, 83
Van Maanen, J., 57, 60
Vocational Rehabilitation Act of 1973, Section 504 of, 28
Volkmann, M. F., 39, 41, 42, 46-47, 50

W

Waldeck, T. A., 72, 82
Washington University, public relations at, 41, 42, 46-47
Waterman, R. H., 85-86, 87
Watson, H. A., 72
Weick, K., 2, 6
West Virginia University, Center for Entrepreneurial Studies at, 58
Western Illinois University, public relations at, 41
Whetten, D. A., 68, 70, 74, 81
White, E. B., 85
White H., 66
William Rainey Harper Community College, nature of, 29
Williamson, E. G., 24
Windham College, and foreign students, 28
Wisconsin, University of, Innovative Service at, 58
Wood, R. K., 78, 83
Worcester Polytechnic Institute, and industry, 58
Wright, C. R., 48, 50

Y

Yale University, and topical self-study, 18